I'm Alive Hurray!

I0378123

Gift Card
Thinking Especially of You

Date:

To:

From:

Message:

© 2018. All Rights Reserved. Esther Tulkoff, I'M ALIVE HURRAY

Congratulations

"Mom
You never cease to amaze us!
Kol hakavod
Much love
L & J"

Love, Lynnette and Jonathan Tulkoff

"We are proud of your
accomplishments and
look forward to reading about
the world according to Bubbe."
Soph and Liv

Love, Sophie Tulkoff

Love, Olivia Tulkoff

Congratulations

"Mom –
Keep living, loving, and laughing.
We r so proud of u."

Love, Donna and Leon Schwechter

(texting shorthand, not a typo)

"Mazel tov Bubby.
May HaShem bless you with
more Yiddishe nachas."

Love, Daniel and Yael Schwechter

Congratulations

"We are so proud of you.
You've been through so much.
We've always been so fortunate
to hear your stories and laugh
and cry with you.

And now the rest of the world
can enjoy your stories too!

We named our beautiful daughter
your great granddaughter
after brilliant Myer,
Meira Malkah, Light and Queen"

Love, Cary and Shuli Schwechter

Congratulations

"Dear Bubby,
We love you so much
and are so proud
to call you our Bubbe!
Writing a book is hard work and
you achieved your goal, and
made your dream come true."

Love, Serena and Ben Kalish

Congratulations

"A great feat has been accomplished."

Dr. Reiner Grabreck, CVE Publish Class

"To Esther
A remarkable lady!
A Bubbe who still thinks like a youngie.
Your book brings much laughter while we still shed some tears. Mazel Tov!"

Judith Rudnick, CVE Publish Class

"Congratulations on publishing your book. I know how hard it is to have the discipline to complete the very difficult task of writing a book. You set a very good example for all of us to achieve by publishing your book."

Richard Herrick, CVE Publish Class

© 2018. All Rights Reserved. Esther Tulkoff, I'M ALIVE HURRAY

Congratulations

"I wish you much Hatzlacha
in everything you do.
And you should be well to
enjoy everything."

Ellen Brander, CVE Publish Class

"Great job!
You proved that every day
is a new beginning."

Ruth Rosenberg, CVE Publish Class

"Congratulations, Esther.
It couldn't happen to a nicer person."

Shoshana Caplan, CVE Publish Class

© 2018. All Rights Reserved. Esther Tulkoff, I'M ALIVE HURRAY

Congratulations

"Congratulations Esther on the publication of your book. Hurray Esther Tulkoff!"

Mary Moss, CVE Publish Class

"Hurray Esther, Congratulations on your wonderful, heartwarming book! You are a pleasure to know."

Maria Sakowitz, CVE Publish Class

Congratulations! Wonderful!

Dr. Jerry Gray, CVE Publish Class

© 2018. All Rights Reserved. Esther Tulkoff, I'M ALIVE HURRAY

Congratulations

"I'm 82 years old. I'm absolutely thrilled that Esther is starting a new chapter and made her dream come true. I adore it."

Shula Cohen, CVE Class Guest

"Congratulations Esther! It's amazing to see you fulfill your dream."

Kimberly Dove and CVE Daytime Staff
CVE Information Office

© 2018. All Rights Reserved. Esther Tulkoff, I'M ALIVE HURRAY

Congratulations

After 7 years of phone calls to your family about the doctor, diagnosis, disease, dying and death, you triumphed over tragedy: **Mortality.**

You came to my publishing class with a few handwritten notes scribbled on a yellow legal pad. 75% of the class had 15-25 year old manuscripts ready to publish. Your book is the first to be published. How did you do it? Especially with excruciatingly painful arthritis! You are a published "authoritis."

From A-Z, you followed every instruction. Your beautiful book is a flawless example that showcases how a digital book is written, edited, published, marketed, and sold in less than a year: **Digital Immortality!**

In your twilight years, you found a literary passion and made one more dream come true. Every phone call home will be about your literary readings, book clubs, book sales, fan club, arthritic autographs, and Epson salt baths.

You are about to set sail on an exciting new journey of sharing your funny stories with the world, on a global scale.

Make Everyone Laugh, Keep Everyone Happy!

Sharon Esther Lampert
Teacher, CVE Publish Class
Class: Publish Book in 30 Days

I'M ALIVE HURRAY!

© 2018. All Rights Reserved. Esther Tulkoff, I'M ALIVE HURRAY

I'M ALIVE HURRAY!
Overcoming Life's Obstacles with Laughter and Love

A Memoir

Esther Tulkoff

 iPublishUGlobal   Florida   2018

© 2018. All Rights Reserved. Esther Tulkoff, I'M ALIVE HURRAY

I'M ALIVE HURRAY
Copyright ©2018, ©2019 by Esther Tulkoff

All rights reserved. Published in the United States by
iPublishUGlobal.com
World's Only Full Service Publisher
Write, Dictate, Edit, Publish, Market, and Sales
Florida
www.iPublishUGlobal.com

ISBN: 978-1-885872-19-7 (paperback)
PCN: 2018953833 (memoir)

All rights reserved. No part of this publication may be reproduced, stored in a retrieval system, or transmitted in any form or by any means—electronic, mechanical, photocopy, recording, or any other—except for brief quotations in printed reviews, without the prior written permission of the author.

Cover and Book Design by Creative Genius Sharon Esther Lampert
www.sharonestherlampert.com

Thank you Steve Jobs for my MAC AIR computer
"A Light Shines in the Garden of Eden"

Manufactured in the United States of America
First Edition

Dedication

For Future Generations

I plan to live forever inside this digital book, and tell short stories to my family, friends, and fans on a global scale for millenniums.

With Laughter and Love,

Esther Tulkoff

Website: www.esthertulkoff.com
Email: esther@esthertulkoff.com

© 2018. All Rights Reserved. Esther Tulkoff, I'M ALIVE HURRAY

Epigraph

*If you would not be forgotten
as soon as you are dead and rotten
either write something worth reading
or do things worth writing.*

Benjamin Franklin

Table of Contents

Table of Contents

Timeline of Esther Tulkoff 1

Prologue 2
Am I Embarrassing You? 3

Introduction 4
Mishpacha and Naches 5

Childhood 14
How to Fly a Plane 15
Nun No, Ashes Yes 17

Marriage 20
My Bashert's Brother Eats Grass 21
Mine Knows How to Fix Cars 25
My First Fur Jacket 26
How Funny Honey Is That? 27
Jackie Onassis and Me 31
Tzedakah Beauty Parlor 37

Children 42
Prophetess Hannah and Me 43

Teacher 46
Morah Tulkoff and G-D 47
Beautiful Blue Eyes 49
A Light Shines in the Garden of Eden 51
Kisses for Everyone 53

Daisy Chihuahua Tulkoff   *56*
Bless You Rabbi Tendler   57

Family   *58*
Warsaw Father, Vishkava Mother   59
You Never Did Forget   65
My Beloved Only Sister Reva   69
Sisters-In-Law: Zelda, Rosalie, and Ruth   71

Beloved Family Photos   *76*
- Esther Tulkoff High School Graduation   77
- Esther Tulkoff Modeling Photo   78
- Esther Tulkoff Modeling Photo   79
- Tulkoff Family   80
  Couch: Esther, Mother, Father, Uncle Avram, Brother Solomon
  Floor: Brother Teddy, Sister Reva, Cousin Max
- Colonel Myer Tulkoff, US Army   81
- Esther and Myer Tulkoff Wedding, March 7, 1953   82
- Last Cruise, Esther and Myer Tulkoff   83
- Wedding: Esther and Mother, March 7, 1953   84
- Wedding: Esther and Myer, Mother, Father, and Grandfather   85
- Esther, Myer, and Daisy Tulkoff   86
- Daisy Chihuahua Tulkoff Drives a Buick   87

- Myer Tulkoff Dedication Bench Plaque, Florida 88
- Esther Tulkoff, I'M ALIVE HURRAY, Florida 89

Beloved Family Letters   91
- Rabbi Nachum Muschel 92, 93
- Aide Ann Marie Treasure 94
- Joe DiMaggio Children's Hospital Foundation 95
- Young Israel of Deerfield Beach and Israel Bonds 96, 97
- Beauty School License 98, 99
- Original Handwritten Manuscript: "Jonathan" 100, 101

Retirement   104
Who Died Today? 105

Alzheimers Disease   108
Hey Kids: Myer and Mary 109
I Love You Too! 113
Dr. Drek 117
I'm Going to Jail, 119
Myer's Birthday Cupcakes & 15 Stitches 125

The Angel of Death Knocks on Two Doors   128
One Finger Miracle Alert 129
Misdiagnosis, Fistfight, Finger Nerve Endings, Neck Neurosurgery, and Myer Goes to Hospice 135
I Will Always Love You 139
Missed Myer's Funeral (Dec 10, 2015) 145

© 2018. All Rights Reserved. Esther Tulkoff, I'M ALIVE HURRAY

The Angel of Death Won't Let Go of Me!   150
Dr. Gonif: What Did You Do? 151
3 Weeks of Malpractice: Treatment Before Diagnosis 159
Five Hours of Poison Injections 161
I'm So Disgusted, I Can't Even Talk About It! 165

I'm Alive Hurray   170
I Love That Line 171

Epilogue   176
Thanking G-D and Leon for Help 177

Appendix: 182
Bubbe Esther's Daily Action Plan 184-185
Bubbe Esther's Self-Help 186-187
Thank You Toyota Norman Frantz 188-189
Bubbe Esther's Gluten-Free Shabbat Cholent 190-191
Join Our Short Story Writer's Club 192-193

Last Will & Testament Digital Assets   201

© 2018. All Rights Reserved. Esther Tulkoff, I'M ALIVE HURRAY

Disclaimer

Some names and identifying details have been changed to protect the privacy of individuals.

Fair Use Notice

The copyrighted material, namely quotes,
the use of which has not always been specifically
authorized by the copyright owner.

We are making such material available in our
efforts to advance understanding of
issues of humanitarian significance.

We believe this constitutes a 'fair use' of
any such copyrighted material as provided
for in section 107 of the US Copyright Law.

When an old person dies, a library is lost.

Tommy Swan

Timeline of Esther Tulkoff

- Born in Kentucky
- Educated in Baltimore and New York
- My father was a Jewish Orthodox Rabbi and Schochet
- My mother passed away when I was twenty-five years of age
- I was one of 6 siblings: 2 girls, 4 boys, I am number 3
- Met my husband Myer in Baltimore
- Myer passed the Bar in Kentucky and New York City
- Myer was a Full Colonel in the U.S. Army
- Myer was President of Community Synagogue of Monsey, Rockland County, N.Y.
- My Tulkoff family practiced Modern Jewish Orthodoxy
- Raised a family of two, Donna and Jonathan, in New York State
- Two beloved pets: cat Marmalade and dog Daisy
- 5 Grandchildren and 3 In-Law Grandchildren, by Marriage
- 6 Great Grandchildren
- 1 adopted grandaughter, Sharon Esther Lampert (also my publisher)
- Taught kindergarten for 30 years
- Beauty school graduate and licensed beautician
- Visited Israel many times
- Retired in Florida

I'M ALIVE HURRAY

Prologue

Prologue

Am I Embarrassing You?

Children figure out what you will do before you do it sometimes. I heard Donna whisper to Lynnette in the restaurant,
"Just watch, she's going to take the food she doesn't finish home. I'm so embarrassed."
I said out loud, "Listen, my mother embarrassed me. I will embarrass you, and you can embarrass your children." They didn't think it was so funny, but I think it was!

Bubbe Esther Tulkoff

*Bubbe (Yiddish: Grandmother)

I'M ALIVE HURRAY

Introduction

Introduction

Mishpacha and Naches*

What I have to tell you is that I can say I'm still alive. I am so lucky because I have two children Donna and Jonathan and at times, I almost put them up for adoption.

I have five grandchildren: Donna's children are Daniel, Cary and Serena. Jonathan's children are Sophie and Olivia.

I am also blessed with four great grandchildren: Sima, Raizel, Ella, and Roey. I love and enjoy them all.

What I have to tell you is that I can say I'm still alive because I have a wonderful son-in-law, Dr. Leon Schwechter who is married to my wonderful daughter Donna.

I'M ALIVE HURRAY

They have three children Daniel, a Rabbi with Smicha (Yiddish: a Rabbi's diploma) from Yeshiva University, married to my darling Yael Wienokur who became a lawyer when she had two little kids. They now have three beautiful girls Sima, eight, Raizel, six, Ella, three, and I love them all dearly. Yael is a beautiful, wonderful, and bright mother and daughter-in-law. I love her dearly too!

Cary, my darling second grandson, the social worker married to Shulie Rosen, whom I love so much because she is beautiful, smart, talented, and a wonderful girl. They have one little boy, Roey, two years old, who is the most wonderful child in the world, I think.

Serena was the answer to Donna's wish to have a girl, and she is a blessing to the whole family. She is a physician's assistant and is married to Ben Kalish, an attorney with the U.S. Securities and Exchange Commission. I loved him the minute I met him.

My son Jonathan Tulkoff is a very successful businessman. He is married to Lynnette Luyt Tulkoff. The most beautiful, talented, successful real estate professional, and wonderful mother and cook.

Jonathan travels all over the world but tries to be home for the Sabbath. He is well known in the Jewish and business world. I love him so so much. He and his family lived in Israel for a year. Mr. Bigshot, call your mother more than once a week!

They have two daughters. Sophie, 23, beautiful and very smart. She graduated from SAR Yeshiva in NY, and went into the IDF (Israel Defense Forces.) She was liaison to Jordan. John Hopkins University held a spot for her, and she graduated with a business degree in international studies.

She is a feminist and activist for the rights of women. Recently, I sent her a t-shirt with big letters saying, **"GIRL POWER."** She texted back a photo wearing it. I told her she looked gorgeous, and sent her my love.

When she first arrived at the IDF, she called me and said, "Bubbe, you won't believe this! There are five Shomer Shabbos girls in my troop!"

I could only think to say, "Isn't that nice!"

When she came back from IDF, I asked her, " What did you do as a liaison to Jordan?

I'M ALIVE HURRAY

She said, "I could tell you, but I would have to shoot you!"

I said, "Don't tell me."

Olivia, the second daughter, is also very beautiful, talented, and very bright. After also graduating from SAR Yeshiva, she went to IDF in Israel, and was trained to teach the soldiers to shoot. She is still in Israel and Brown University is holding a spot for her.

Personalities and wonderful nachas they all have, which means I have nachas from all their children, grandchildren, and great grandchildren. I think its wonderful when I receive texts and emails from many of them. But they can be pretty funny because they are a different generation. I asked my grandchild Olivia,

"Who are you talking to on the computer?"

She said, "My friend Judy."

I said, "Doesn't she live right next door?"

I said, "Why don't you go to talk to her there?"

She said, "Oh, I don't have to!"

And I do have to remember my little five pound dog, Daisy, a Chihuahua, whom Myer and I loved very much and who loved us very much. The first time Myer took a bath in the jacuzzi, it was on Sunday morning, and he could not get up to get out.

He yelled, "Esther, Esther, I need help!"

I went in and said, "What day is it?"

He said, "Sunday." I said, "Oh, I'll, be back on Tuesday."

He said, "Cut it out, help me!"

I said, "I just want you to know that if you and Daisy are drowning, you better grab her because she is the one I'm saving."

He said, "I hope you're kidding."

I said, "Yes, I am."

Daisy passed away at age thirteen and a half years old from old age, in my arms, rushing to the vet. I always carried her in my purse everywhere I could take her. Daisy became a very big part of my life.

I met Myra Crane when I was out with my cousin, a Chasidisha nice looking lady, as we tried to sell our promotional products.

I'M ALIVE HURRAY

We walked into a customer who looked at us and said,

"Ladies, I am going to buy some of your products," but first, as he looked at me in a nice short skirt and a fancy top, he asked,

"Just tell me how did you two get together?"

And Daisy was in my arms. I told him we were cousins. I don't know what he thought, but he was pleasant.

As we walked out, we met a beautiful woman and her beautiful mother. She stopped me and asked if she could get together with a little dog, for doggy dates as her vet told her to try to introduce her new little dog, Zena, to interplay with other dogs. She was a June Taylor dancer on the Jackie Gleason show for three years. She was beautiful. After deciding to get together, I invited her to come to my house in Monsey, N.Y. so in case she thought our house was not good enough for her because she lived in Upper Saddle River Road, a wealthy community. We made a date, and I told

Myer that a beautiful woman was coming with her dog. He could look but he must not touch. She walked in with her Mother and her husband, and we became best of friends, even till today.

* Mishpacha: Hebrew for family
* Naches: Yiddish for pride

Literature Is Powerful Beyond Words For It Creates Worlds

Sharon Esther Lampert
Poet, Philosopher, Peacemaker, Prophet

I'M ALIVE HURRAY

Childhood

How to Fly a Plane

I was born in Louisville Kentucky. I had two older brothers born in Poland, and I was the first child born in America. My sister and two younger brothers made us six siblings: Abe, Solomon, Me (Esther), Reva, Max, and Teddy. We were pretty happy kids.

We were allowed to play outside without reporting where we were going, as long as we were home for dinner, and got ready for bed. Nobody at that time worried that someone would be in danger playing with friends and going from place to place.

When I turned about thirteen, I was friends with some nice kids who found that if we could say we were fifteen, we could join the Civil Air Patrol, and learn how to fly a plane.

One of the other parents arranged it all and it was so much fun. I did not tell my folks what I was doing, but my father was a Rabbi and we were Sabbath observers.

I'M ALIVE HURRAY

I needed his signature to go up in a two-seater plane on a Saturday. When he read the paper to sign, he could not believe it. He was shocked! But I cried and begged him to let me go.

He said, "You could get killed on a plane!"

I said, "So you will have one less kid to take care of!"

He said, "It is before Passover, and I don't have time for a funeral!"

I begged him, and he finally agreed that he would call, and see if he could bring me on Sunday. So he drove me to the airport, and I went up in the back seat of the plane, and was shown how to maneuver the plane from the back seat. I loved going up, but I came down so sick and nauseous, that I never wanted go on a plane again. My father was so happy!

Nun No, Ashes Yes

I went to public school and chedar (Yiddish: Hebrew school) until my parents permitted me to go to Bais Yakov, a Jewish Theological Seminary at 141 South Third Street, in the Williamsburg district of Brooklyn, for the last two years of high school.

If I had known that I had to take Regents tests in New York to get a diploma, I don't know if I would have gone to Seminary.

I lived with three girls in Mrs. Kaplan's apartment who rented rooms (She was such a yenta!) We shared the kitchen and the bathroom. We each had our own room. My parents paid for my room, and I worked in a doctor's office to pay my living expenses while I was going to school.

One evening, she came to my room, and said to me, "Hob Ich For Dir, Aza Shaina, Aza Finer, Gutta

I'M ALIVE HURRAY

Boy, Ober Ain Zach, Er Hut Peyes Ober Er Gait It Arum The Eeren, Mir Ken Nit Zayn."
Translation: "I have such a beauty for you. A fine boy. A good boy. Only one thing. He has peyes, but it is around his ears and you really can't see them."

I said, "Thank you very much but I am not interested." She was not happy with my answer.

I took the Regents tests, passed, and got my diploma and stayed in seminary for a teacher's degree.

In those days, they allowed me to do two years of schooling in one and I did. So I graduated quite young at age sixteen.

I returned to Baltimore, where my family had moved, and I went to college to get early childhood certification. I got very friendly there with Peggy, not Jewish, and she loved coming to my house and family and I would go to her house.

When she was thinking to become a Nun her mother asked me to please get her to not do it.

I remember how when we were in college together we were walking on Good Friday, and I knew that her Mother wanted her to get ashes on her forehead. She was not excited to do that, but I influenced her to do it.

She ultimately got married, and we lost touch with each other until many years later when she looked me up. I arranged to meet her in Delaware, where she lived and we had coffee together. We were driving from N.Y. to Baltimore to visit with my family. That was the last time I saw her.

I heard my school had a fire and that was why I could not get my records. They were destroyed. Later, I found the article about the fire posted on an online newspaper, as follows:

TWO FIRES DAMAGE JEWISH SEMINARY
800 Students Evacuated From Brooklyn School
Search for Pyromaniac Started
New York Times

I used to say while walking up and down the steps in the school, "This is so dangerous, this place is going to burn down!" And so it did! **OY VEY!**

I'M ALIVE HURRAY

Marriage

My Bashert's Brother Eats Grass

I was in Baltimore for a week from New York when I met Mrs. Tulkoff from Kentucky. She was visiting the Tulkoffs our next door neighbors. She told me about her son, the lawyer, and she told him about the Rabbi's daughter. She asked me to look up her younger son, Milton, who was in, Torah Vadas Yeshiva, near the seminary. So I did and took him out to eat. He had such a real southern accent.

When I asked him what he would like to eat, he said, "Grass."

I said, "Grass?"

He said, "No, I mean rice."

I had to say I was related for the principal to allow Milton to go with me. Shortly after that, her son the lawyer Myer called me to meet me in New York. I would never think to go out with a hillbilly while I was at seminary.

I'M ALIVE HURRAY

I said, "I am going back to Baltimore for a few days. If you can visit your aunt and uncle, we could go out."

He showed up in a taxi on the Sabbath. It is lucky that my parents thought he came from next door.

So I told him, "I do not travel on the Sabbath." And he suggested, that we could walk in the woods in the back of our houses and talk and get to know each other. Meanwhile, I was dating a young guy Rob who was not religious, but we liked each other. But I could not think that I would marry him, and I told him so. He was a chemist and assured me, I could be religious, but he could not. He had to work on Saturday.

But Myer, on the other hand, during our walk, kept assuring me that he had always wanted to be religious, and was so happy to be with me. We spent the day just getting to know each other.

After my father, who liked Myer right away, offered to let us use his car after the Sabbath, we drove around Baltimore for a while. He in his army uniform that made him look so good and he was telling me that he was going to Korea next week. He alluded that maybe we could go away together before he went.

    I assured him that, "I would never travel overnight with a guy unless we were married."

    He said, "Maybe that is what we should do?"

    I said, "Maybe?"

    When I got home, I told my father that I was going to marry him. I got the feeling that he thought that might be a good idea.

    When he told my mother, she said,

    "What? she is going to marry a soldier, a bum!"

    My father calmed her down.

    The next morning, when Myer came over to my house, my father asked him to sit and talk about his background in learning, Yiddishkeit. He gave him a siddur and a Jewish book of laws of the Jewish religion. Myer liked that (Yiddish: siddur is a Jewish prayerbook).

    Later, I asked him if we really should get married. He said, "We are now engaged."

    That night, Myer and I were on the porch and Shlomo my brother came out to make sure nothing would happen between us, and just kept talking about anything...

I'M ALIVE HURRAY

And Myer finally said that he was tired and went back next door. He was visiting his aunt and uncle. When I went upstairs to bed, Shlomo came in and told me,

"You had some nerve to keep me up so late."

I answered, "Who asked you to stay?"

We got engaged, and he went to Korea. We corresponded that whole year. I still have many of the letters we sent to each other.

We had a small engagement party before he left. And I had an engagement ring. My father did not allow me to sign engagement papers because if he was killed in Korea, I would be considered a widow.

So when he left, I signed up and made a folder to do modeling. I have one modeling photo.

Mine Knows How to Fix Cars

Shortly after we got married, Miriam and Abe Tous and Bea and David Lewis and Myer and, I went for a ride in Myer's car, and it stalled.

The car had a hole in the back on the floor. And everyone was advised to keep their feet off the floor. In those days, six people sat comfortably in a car. His was an old Dodge, but I did love that car.

The men got out, opened the hood and tried to start it. It was so cold. Finally I remembered that my father taught me how to start a stalled car. So I got out and opened the carburetor and emptied it and got back into the car.

I told the guys that it was fixed. So they got back in and the car started. When we got back to the apartment, he was mad. And said, "Everyone else's wife knew how to cook! Mine knows how to fix cars!" I said, "You should thank me. You would have been frozen!" Miriam and I are still best friends, and we still laugh when we talk about it.

I'M ALIVE HURRAY

My First Fur Jacket

When Donna was about three years old, I was getting black and blue marks up and down my arms, and some on my body. This went on for some time.

Eventually, I did go to a doctor. He saw something on the lungs on my x-ray. He took a biopsy. In those days, it took a week to ten days to get results. I was convinced that I was dying of cancer. I thought to myself, that I had worked very hard my whole life, so I was not going to make it easy for the second Mrs. Tulkoff.

So I began to charge everything I desired, including a fur jacket. Myer was such a wonderful man, and he allowed me to do that. By the time I found out that I did not have cancer, it was a little late. It took us three years to pay off the credit cards.

I did find out that I had Sarcoidosis and not cancer, and the Sarcoidosis had healed itself. To this day, I still check at least once a year to be sure that the disease is not active or effecting my eyes.

How Funny Honey Is That?

Myer, my husband was assistant regional director of the Federal Trade Commission for about fifteen years, and was an officer in the U.S. Army Reserves for approximately twenty-eight years. He went up in rank to Full Colonel and second in command of 600 troops. He also served in the U.S. Army in Japan and Korea. He was also antitrust counsel to AT&T for twenty years.

    We were Sabbath observers. We both got married knowing that was our way of life. It was not easy as he was not a chaplain. He and the Chaplain Abe Averich, would go to the Armory once a month on Friday evenings, sleep there, and come home either Saturday night or Sunday morning so they did not travel on the Sabbath. His wife and I sent them food for the Sabbath.

    I often had to go with him to military balls on Friday and stay at Fort Hamilton. Occasionally we had to stay in hotels so we did not have to travel on the Sabbath.

I'M ALIVE HURRAY

We came into the Armory before the Sabbath, and as we walked in we heard two soldiers talking,

"We have to press Colonel Tulkoff's wife's dress before the sun goes down."

Its like they all knew we were religious but not what it was all about. I laughed and said to Myer,

"How funny honey is that?"

We were able to adjust so we would keep the Sabbath wherever we were. It was not easy.

Long before I had any connection to Great Neck, Long Island, Leonard's Banquet Hall held a military ball on a Friday night. We tried to find a place to stay over night so we could walk to the hall. There were no hotels or motels nearby then. I remembered that my friend's sister and brother-in-law moved to Great Neck at least ten years earlier. Diane and Herbie Kalter were lovely people. I called them and said,

"Hi Diane. This is Esther Tulkoff. Do you remember me?

It had been at least ten years that we had not been in touch with each other.

She said, "Yes, how nice to hear from you."

I said, "Guess who's coming for Shabbos, if you let us come?" She was delighted and we had a wonderful Shabbos* together.

***Shabbos** is Yiddish for the Jewish Sabbath
 Shabbat is Hebrew for the Jewish Sabbath

I'M ALIVE HURRAY

Jackie Onassis and Me

Myer was the assistant regional director of the Federal Trade Commission (FTC) of the north east section of the country. We had many exciting things happen when he was with the FTC.

Myer was on the radio as a hearing attorney for the agency, a few times and we always listened and taped the programs. My daughter Donna was then going to a Yeshiva High School in NYC and Myer would drive some girls to and from school. Sometimes, he was on the program, and had to pick the girls up from school and the program was not over.

He would say, "I have to turn this hearing over to my assistant, as I have to be at another appointment."

I'M ALIVE HURRAY

I knew that his appointment was to pick up the girls in the carpool from school. It was then that I realized that everything in the news was not necessarily exactly true. He was written up in the newspaper about being a great investigator and a great consumer protector.

As part of the life of a military wife, I had many wonderful experiences that we were invited to be part of.

Myer and the general were good friends. His wife, Mimi, and I were also very friendly. We chaired a military ball at the Statler Hilton Hotel in New York City together. We were invited to one of the Kennedy Inaugural Balls.

We were seated in the second row in front of the stage. I am sure that it was a fluke. But it was such a great program and show. I have never forgotten it.

It was a few years later when we had another connection to the Kennedy family again. I have never seen so many beautiful people together, as the Kennedy and the Ladybird family.

The shows that we saw there were the best shows we've ever seen. I saved all the programs and all the articles from that wonderful time. I stored them in a little cabinet in the basement. Myer was home one day on a holiday, but I had to go to school that day. He thought that he could help me.

So he called the Salvation Army to come and take the cabinet away. He did not empty the cabinet so they took everything in the cabinet with them. I was so upset. We tried to get them back. But they never returned them to us, and didn't allow us to find them. Somebody took them. I have always been upset about that and I was really upset that he let them take it.

I also remember that I thought I was the only lady in the audience that did not wear a fur coat. So eventually I did get a fur coat. I did get a few calls from friends that saw us, sitting in the audience, in newspapers.

I'M ALIVE HURRAY

It was a few years later when we had a connection to the Kennedy family again. Myer had become a full colonel in military government and was second in command of 600 troops. He and the general, the commander, were invited to the Metropolitan Opera House to meet Jackie Kennedy. We wives were also invited. She was the most beautiful woman, with such an aura that I have ever met. She was very thin and striking looking. She spoke very softly.

There was a reception line to meet her and she greeted everyone. Myer went first and she spoke to him in almost a whisper. He was wearing his dress uniform with his name tag on it.

She spoke so softly, "It's so nice to meet you Colonel Tulkoff."

And then she addressed me in a whispered voice and said, "Its so nice to meet you Mrs. Tulkoff."

I really wanted to yell, "What?"

But Myer looked at me with that look,

"Don't you dare!"

If we had the computer then, that we now have, that would have been great to put on Twitter.

I'M ALIVE HURRAY

Tzedakah* Beauty Parlor

After Myer and I got married and we had two kids, I decided to take a course in a beauty school, because I was not happy anymore with the beautician that was doing my hair for a few years.

I lived close to the beauty school and I signed up when the kids were away and I was free for summer vacation.

I met my very closest friend Renee Kadan. We both were the oldest students in the school. We also each got a beautician's license.

It was like a new world to me.

I had not been in that kind of atmosphere, where the students were from a different kind of society from the kind of life I lived.

Beauty school was a broadening experience for me.

I'M ALIVE HURRAY

I remember when a group of students and I were talking to each other, they were discussing how long each was married. They all were married about three to seven years. One asked,

"Esther, how long are you married?"

I answered, "Twenty-five years."

"To the same guy?"

I had also been introduced to marijuana. I went to the ladies room and there was a funny smell. I asked the girls there what the smell was. They told me. It was the first time and the last time I ever smelled marijuana.

I learned how to do nails, hair, make-up, facials, massage and waxing. I loved doing it.

I set up a beauty parlor in my basement, and I had ladies come to me when I was home from school.

It was fun for me. I would not let them pay me, but I would put the money into a TZEDAKAH box (Hebrew: charity).

Alot of the parents at the school that I taught came for beauty treatments. Sue, Rachel, and Florence came regularly.

Myer did not like to come home to find me busy with ladies. He finally said, I should not have ladies in our house when he came home from work.

So I had to close shop.

But it was fun while it lasted.

I still have my beautician's license.

(See Beloved Family Letters).

And Renee and I have been closest friends even to today. We get together very often and have always kept in touch.

My TZEDAKAH beauty parlor made women beautiful, and made contributions to a more beautiful world: TIKKUN OLAM.*

*TIKKUN OLAM: Hebrew for Repairing the World

I'M ALIVE HURRAY

Crushed in soul, Hannah prayed to God
and cried and cried—inconsolably.

Then she made a vow:

Oh, God-of-the-Angel-Armies,

If you'll take a good, hard look at my pain,

If you'll quit neglecting me and go into action for me

By giving me a son,

I'll give him completely, unreservedly to you.

I'll set him apart for a life of holy discipline.

Prophets, Samuel 1, 9-11

I'M ALIVE HURRAY

Children

Prophetess Hannah and Me

Jonathan was born when Donna was six years old. When we did not have another child in 5 years, I went to a gynocologist, and after an exam, he told me, that I was what they called a "one child sterility case." I was upset, but I told myself that I had to thank G-D that I had such a beautiful daughter and I should thank G-D for what I considered the biggest blesssing in the world.

After a few weeks of kind of adjusting to this, I finally decided to give her carriage and stroller to charity. That was when I became pregnant with Jonathan. Myer and I were so delighted to add a son to our family. We felt we should name him Jonathan - which comes from the Hebrew word, "Hashem Natan" (Hashem has given). We had to buy new baby necessities. We felt so lucky.

I'll bet today, I would have given birth to a litter if placed on modern day fertility drugs.

I'M ALIVE HURRAY

Darling Oprah,
Your quote introduces my vignettes as a teacher.
This tribute to you is to pay forward my respects
to you in gratitude for all you have taught me.
Laughter and Love,
Esther Tulkoff

Oprah's Life and Legacy
- Millions (Global Reach) of MITZVOT* for Humanity for Generations
- **CHUTZPAH AWARD** (Yiddish: Guts, Balls, or Moxie)
- Presidential Medal of Freedom
- Kennedy Center Honors
- Thirty-nine Daytime Emmy Awards
- Self-Made Woman Billionaire

Oprah's Traumatic Childhood and Adulthood
- Raped: age 9, Molested: ages 10-14 and Whipped
- Institutionalized Racism in America: Birth - Present (Excerpt from book, "Note to Self," Pages 9-10)

* MITZVOT: Yiddish for Good Deeds

The great courageous act that we must all do, is to have the courage to step out of our history and past so that we can live our dreams.

Oprah

Spiritual Teacher, Talk-Show Host, and Humanitarian

I'M ALIVE HURRAY

Teacher

Morah* Tulkoff and G-d

I was a kindergarten teacher for 30 years in HIROC Yeshiva, which became ASHAR Yeshiva of Monsey, N.Y. I loved working with kindergarten-age children and can say each and every child in every one of my classes has a special place in my heart.

A few years ago, I was at a wedding, when a young man said, "Morah* Tulkoff?"

I turned and said, "Yes!"

He said, "Do you remember me?"

I said, "I think I do."

He said, "Don't go away. I will be right back."

In about 2-3 minutes, he came back with a cute little girl about 4 or 5 years old, and said to the little girl,

"Tell her who I always say is the best teacher I ever had."

I'M ALIVE HURRAY

In her cute little voice, she said, "Mrs. Tulkoff." And I said, "Barry, you were like that in kindergarten, and it seems that you are still like that, and I still love you!"

I do still have some contact with some of them, as they have grandparents here that are part of Young Israel of Deerfield Beach. Many visit with their children. I have so much NACHES when I see how wonderful they have grown up, and have families of their own.

One call was so endearing, A mother called me at home because her daughter said she could not nap on Rosh Hashanah. She must go to a lake or river to throw away her sins because Morah Tulkoff and G-d said she should. I spoke to her daughter, and said she could go to the river or lake and then take a nap.

I wish I had a list of all the kids from records at school. Maybe 600-700 children? I think I remember them all more or less, and I'd love to hear from them. How they are, and where they are in their life today. (*Morah is Hebrew for teacher)

Beautiful Blue Eyes

My associate teacher Sylvia, took one class in the morning and we traded for the afternoon. I would take the class she had in the morning.

Every time for a few weeks, I would pass her room and see one of the boys, Nathan, and saw that she picked on that child. I thought I must save him. He was always sitting in the corner by himself, in her room, and I saw him there.

I called her out and said, "I have to talk to you. What's the story about him?"

She said, "I cannot stand him. There is nothing I like about him."

I said, "Look at his beautiful blue eyes."

She said, "I never noticed them."

I replied, "You better look at his eyes every time you talk to him."

I'M ALIVE HURRAY

I followed up, and she did stop picking on him so much. She had the principal fooled. It was really sad that she could feel that way about any child. She was quite nasty after that and created some problems for me, but I laughed it off. I told jokes about it to other teachers.

This young man has become a great Rabbi. Kinehora!*

I never told his parents.

*Kinehora! Yiddish: Ward off the evil eye.

A Light Shines in the Garden of Eden

We were honored at Young Israel at Deerfield Beach with a magnificent dinner.

Rabbi Nachum Muschel and his wife did attend and we were so happy that they were there. He even addressed the audience and spoke beautifully about us, my husband, and myself.

He passed away a few years ago.

I have many fond memories of my principal, Rabbi Nachum Muschel, who I liked and very much appreciated that he was a wonderful and brilliant administrator.

I always appreciated his notes, thanking me for my programs and plays that I did every year with every class. I even now feel that wonderful feeling of accomplishment. May Hashem grant you Rabbi Nachum Muschel a Lichtegen Gan Eden (Yiddish: a brightness in the Garden of Eden).

Even after I retired, he sent me this last beautiful letter (see Beloved Letters).

I'M ALIVE HURRAY

Kisses for Everyone

I have been receiving texts from Sammy Billel, who is about fifty years old today, but I never really returned an acknowledgement to his texts.

Recently I noticed a nice text and I sent a text back saying that I was glad to hear from him and asking him about his parents, who we were friendly with, and how was his brother who was also in my class the next year. They were both lovely boys.

Flashback: I had not thought about an episode in the kindergarten when he was in my class. A little girl was in line when she accidentally bumped into him causing him to fall. He started to turn blue and looked like he could not breathe. I reacted immediately - picked him up and blew as hard as I could until he caught his breath.

I'M ALIVE HURRAY

The children were saying what happened to Sammy? I answered, I just felt like kissing him. Would anybody else like a kiss? All twenty-seven kids got into line for a kiss.

As soon as I could get a teacher to cover my class, I raced to the principal's office. I was so upset because I did not have an assistant in my class that would have allowed me to get help if I needed it.

He could see that I was so upset and said,

"If he died than you would get an assistant."

"I want one before it happens!"

He did hire an assistant, Ahuvah, who worked with me for more than ten years.

Sammy's mother who worked in the school caferteria forgot to tell me that he was asthmatic.

Fast forward: When Sammy got my text, he called my beloved daughter Donna to ask for my phone number. He called me and I was delighted to hear from him. He does not live far from my apartment.

I invited him to lunch. He reminded me of that episode and said to me,

'I really have to thank you for saving my life!"

He told me all about his family and I had a most delightful afternoon with him. We promised we would get together with his family and he took a picture with me and sent it to his Facebook account.

I have received many lovely texts from my many kindergarten graduates. It was just wonderful.

I'M ALIVE HURRAY

Daisy Chihuahua Tulkoff

Bless You Rabbi Tendler

I would be amiss if I didn't talk about our Rabbi Moshe D. Tendler of Monsey, N.Y., and how much Myer loved and revered him.

Rabbi Tendler always showed his love and appreciation also. I can only say, thank you Rabbi for all your goodness. May HASHEM bless you for all you did for us.

Rabbis generally bless their congregants but I think it is time to bless our Rabbi. His humor was great. One thing that I still remember: I had Daisy and I was a friend of his wife Sifra, and I told her that my father the Rabbi also used to say that a person should not daven (Yiddish: pray) in the same room with an animal.

She must have told him, and in the next sermon he said, "If a person considers his pet as part of the family he is allowed to daven with the pet there."

And I said to Myer, "He's talking to us!"

I'M ALIVE HURRAY

Family

Warsaw Father, Vishkava Mother

My mother was from Vishkava, Poland and my father was from Warsaw, Poland. They lived in Poland until my two older brothers were born. They did go through Ellis Island, though I never heard them talk much about it. I think my mother tried to forget her life there.

She went to school to learn English and my father spoke English well, without going to school. I would always answer any Yiddish questions in English, though I could speak and understand Yiddish, when I was quite young.

My Mother was always sickly, as I remember. She had Diabetes and I measured the insulin and gave her the shots. I don't remember her being a very happy person, but she was loving to us kids. She was always happy to have my friends, and the kids over, and always served nicely when anyone came to our home.

I'M ALIVE HURRAY

My father was always there for us when we came to him. He would walk home rather than spend a nickel on a bus so he could buy us candy.

Sometimes I even remember, as a little girl, getting into bed with one of my parents, as they had separate beds. I do know that we all felt loved.

I do remember that we would come quite often to Baltimore, Myer and I, to visit my parents, and they would often visit us in Forest Hills, N.Y. My friends used to laugh at how we slept on the floor, and gave my parents our beds.

Abruptly, the week after, they came to New Jersey, where we moved a few months earlier, from Forest Hills, for the bris of my son Jonathan. That was the last time I saw my mother, and she looked like herself. I was so glad they were there.

It was exactly three days later, that my father called to tell us that my motherdied, I think from a heart attack. I went to Baltimore for the funeral. I did not take the kids. I try to remember my mom all the time, but I know you can never replace a mother. She and dad always did things for us and were there when we needed them.

My mother died when I was twenty-five years old, from a heart attack. I was already married for seven years. I married very young at the age of twenty and had my daughter Donna right after my first wedding anniversary, on March 7th. She was born on the 24th.

I was walking in Forest Hills one sunny day with her in her carriage. A little old lady stopped me and looked in the carriage at Donna and said,

"What a beautiful baby. Is she yours?"

I said, "Yes." She said,

"She doesn't look at all like you."

"I said, thanks, I think."

My father eventually moved to Cincinnati for a job and married again. His new wife was never married before and really had no family that we knew of. I found an apartment for them in Monsey a few years later to come and live near us but she would not consider it. So I saw very little of my father before he died. We spoke very often on the phone. She was not happy when we wanted to come to visit. After we came to visit,

I'M ALIVE HURRAY

even though she always said to me, not to come, and that it was not a good time to come.

Finally, I said to Myer, "Please lets go so I could spend some time with my father."

When we got to Cincinnati, we called from the airport that we were in Cincinnati and we were coming over. I think she was afraid we might do something. I don't know why? It turned out well. She even insisted that I go with her to her senior center and she took me to meet all of her friends and she introduced me with pride, that I was her daughter. My father was delighted. And we did go a few more times.

My father was very sick but we were able to bring him to Jonathan's Bar-Mitzvah. He passed away soon after.

We took care of his new wife after he died. Sol my brother lived closer to her. So he was able to look after her until she died.

I never met my grandmothers or one grandfather. I only met my mother's father a few times in New York as he had remarried, and his new wife wanted no part of us kids. She had her own kids that we never met.

I'M ALIVE HURRAY

You Never Did Forget

My wonderful mother-in-law, Sophie, and father-in-law, Robert, were very much a part of our family. We brought them from Kentucky to Monsey, N.Y. when my father-in-law got sick. He was taken to the hospital to be examined. He was under my friend's care, a doctor of Proctology, and he put my father-in-law into the hospital.

But he got even sicker there and a day later I went to visit by myself during my lunch hour from school and I saw that he was desperately ill. I asked the nurses if the doctor had seen him? They said, "No."

So I called the doctor at his house and told him that he better get over to my father-in-law ASAP! He is very very sick. Its lucky I came to the hospital at lunch time to call him. I went back to school. When the doctor got to the hospital, my father-in-law did need surgery immediately for colon cancer.

I'M ALIVE HURRAY

From the hospital, we took him to our home and made Myer's office a hospital room. His sister and her husband and my mother-in-law came and stayed in our home for over a month and a half.

It was a little tight and difficult. At that time, I was preparing for my son Jonathan's Bar-Mitzvah.

I came home from school one afternoon and my Mother-In-Law said to me,

"You know Myer really has only one closet."

I said, "Did you look in all of the closets?"

She said "Yes."

I said, "Were they neat?"

"Yes" She replied.

I said, "That's all that counts!" And started to laugh.

And Myer was in the Army reserve for two weeks. But he did get home in time for the Bar-Mitzvah. I had to care for my father-in-law because my sister-in-law and mother-in-law could not handle it.

I learned how to take care of the colostomy bag he had. For about two and a half months, I came home at lunch to do the cleansing for him and try to handle it so that he was not ashamed. And everybody stayed in my house.

He did say to me when he left to go back to Kentucky, "Honey, you never did forget, Cabade Et Ha-Ah-Bah V'Ha-E-Mah." (Hebrew: Honor your father and mother). We love you!"

But we were able to take him to synagogue for Jonathan's Bar-Mitzvah.

I invited the officers in Myer's unit to the Bar-Mitzvah. Jonathan did a beautiful job reading his Torah portion and making a speech.

One of the officers said to Myer, "I am going right home to straighten my kid out. I know he could never do what Jonathan did so well."

We had officers and Rabbis at the Bar-Mitzvah and everybody seemed to have a great time.

My father-in-law was a very sweet man. My mother-in-law was a very sweet lady too. She loved her children very much. She would say things that could have been insulting, but were really quite funny. She sent a letter before they came and addressed it to, "My wonderful, handsome, bright great man and light of my life, and what's her name?" I still have the letter somewhere. We were already married close to fifteen years.

I'M ALIVE HURRAY

That was just before they came. I did take the letter to school and showed some of the teachers. I really wasn't upset. I thought it was really funny! The teachers were really laughing. I just knew that was her personality. She didn't mean anything bad.

The day before they were supposed to leave, I turned on the dishwasher and lots of smoke came out of the dishwasher. I called the fire department because I thought there was a fire. I ran upstairs to tell them to get up and get out because we have a fire.

My mother-in-law said, "You didn't have to make a fire! We were going home today, anyways."

I said, "I didn't make the fire!

I ran downstairs and when the firemen came, the father of one of my kindergarten students who was a fireman, Joe Katzenstein, started to come in.

I said to him, "Joe, if you ruin anything in my house, your kid may spend another year in kindergarten!" He started to laugh and the fireman found that the cleaning girl had left a plastic bag in the dishwasher. So all ended well, and they went home happy.

My Beloved Only Sister Reva

More than ten years ago, I remember my only sister, one and half years younger than me, Reva, being so sick from Cancer in the hospital in Baltimore where she lived. I lived in New York. I went back and forth to visit with her as much as I could during her last year. When she entered the hospital, I stayed with her for two weeks. I did not go out.

She said, "Esther, move my foot, help my hand, turn me, help me with this or that." I did not leave the hospital for two weeks and slept on two chairs put together. My cousin Deborah Gardin gave me scrubs, the doctor's uniform so I could look like I belonged there. Then I could use their shower.

From there, we went to the hospice together. The night we got there, her husband and two sons met us there. They stayed awhile, and I suggested they go home because I was going to sleep there.

I'M ALIVE HURRAY

They left and I turned around saying,

"Reva, I am putting on pajamas, and I am going to sleep with you."

I turned around and her chest was not going up and down. I started to yell for the nurses.

They finally came in and said, "She is gone."

They asked me, what time, she stopped breathing? I was so upset. I thought they might have come to help me save her. I did not know what to do. Her husband Norman and her sons Baruch and Zvi left. And I could not reach them immediately by phone. I called Myer and a friend, and finally, I got Baruch and Zvi and they came back. The staff took her out. To this day, I miss her. The funny thing is, she always loved my stories. I remember one of the last stories I told her, was the one about the kindergarten kid that would not sleep on Rosh Hashanah. She thought "Morah and G-d" were so funny! She was also a teacher but in the public school system.

Reva was the most wonderful lady, a gutta neshama (Yiddish: a good heart). She was always doing things for other people. I think my children loved her just as I did.

Sisters-In-Law: Zelda, Rosalie, and Ruth

Zelda, Myer's sister, was born and raised in Kentucky, where I am convinced that if you grow up there - you do almost everything slowly. I always felt that she ate so slowly that she would not be finished by the next meal. But I love her dearly. I feel that she is really an angel. She is sweet and caring about everyone.

She dealt so beautifully as she did her best to cope with her husband's Alzheimer's disease till he passed away.

Myer and I used to visit him as often as we could and each time we would leave, Myer would say...

"If that happens to me — shoot me!"

I did not shoot Myer when it happened to him a few years later.

I'M ALIVE HURRAY

Zelda's husband Michael, was a brilliant man. He was a Holocaust survivor and had a strong European accent. She had a strong Southern accent. A conversation in their home sounded like this,

"Huney, coud you taa-ke the suu-gar da-wn?"

He would say, "Ver—uput-It-dar-link?"

Conversations in their home was kind of entertaining. I really love Zelda and before she got married, she and Reva, my sister, of blessed memory, lived in an apartment together for about two years. We all had a great time because the apartment was close to where Myer and I lived in Forest Hills, New York. Zelda and Michael have two wonderful children Nechama "Rose" and David.

Rosalie is married to Milton, Myer's younger brother, who I took out of the Yeshiva for lunch in New York before I met Myer. I always felt that Rosalie and I were not only related, but that we were alike in the way we lived our lives. She became a teacher and we shared many stories about teaching children. Our husbands were brothers, so we could also talk about a few problems that we both experienced. We also often talked politics, and seemed to agree on our political ideas.

Oh, I almost forgot - Milton her husband, worked in Washington in the Pentagon. I truly love and admire Rosalie very much. Rosalie and Milton have two beautiful daughters, Rebekah and Judith Anne.

Ruth was an acquaintance of mine when we were teenagers. I remember her, from before she married my brother Solomon. I always liked her, but we were not what I would call tight friends. I knew she was extremely bright and very nice.

Myer and I got married one and a half years before they did and I will never forget that we were driving from New York to their wedding, in Baltimore, when our car broke down on the way. Donna was a baby, so my brother Sol came to get us and we left our car to be fixed. He was really a little upset that he had to come to get us a few hours before the wedding. It took some time before he stopped complaining about how he knew I would be a pain to him. I did love my brother Sol.

I'M ALIVE HURRAY

Ruth and Sol, my brother, had a daughter, a special child, Aviva. They also have two sons, Yankee and Aaron. They were wonderful as parents.

Aviva did get married and adopted a child Yehuda. She was a very sweet girl. She passed away at age fifty and there was really no way of knowing why. Because autopsy was not allowed in the religious world.

We were all shocked and wish her a Lichtegen Gan Eden (Yiddish: a brightness in the Garden of Eden).

Sol passed away about two or three years later and was buried next to her. Ruth is still caring for Yehuda who was adopted from India by Aviva and her husband Raphael. I love Ruth dearly.

I want you to know that I love each of you best!

I'M ALIVE HURRAY

Beloved Family Photos

Beloved Family Photos

Esther Tulkoff High School Graduation
16 Years Old

© 2018. All Rights Reserved. Esther Tulkoff, I'M ALIVE HURRAY

I'M ALIVE HURRAY

Esther Tulkoff Modeling Photo

© 2018. All Rights Reserved. Esther Tulkoff, I'M ALIVE HURRAY

Beloved Family Photos

Esther Tulkoff Modeling Photo

© 2018. All Rights Reserved. Esther Tulkoff, I'M ALIVE HURRAY

Tulkoff Family

Couch: Esther (age 16) Father, Mother, Uncle Avram, and Brother Solomon
Floor: Brother Teddy, Sister Reva, and Cousin Max

© 2018. All Rights Reserved. Esther Tulkoff, I'M ALIVE HURRAY

Beloved Family Photos

Colonel Myer Tulkoff, U.S. Army

Colonel Myer Tulkoff z"l
10.24.1927-12.10.2015

© 2018. All Rights Reserved. Esther Tulkoff, I'M ALIVE HURRAY

I'M ALIVE HURRAY

Esther and Myer Tulkoff Wedding
March 7, 1953

© 2018. All Rights Reserved. Esther Tulkoff, I'M ALIVE HURRAY

Beloved Family Photos

Esther and Myer Tulkoff
Last Cruise, 2008

© 2018. All Rights Reserved. Esther Tulkoff, I'M ALIVE HURRAY

I'M ALIVE HURRAY

Esther and Mother Betty Rothenberg Tulkoff Wedding, March 7, 1953

© 2018. All Rights Reserved. Esther Tulkoff, I'M ALIVE HURRAY

Beloved Family Photos

Standing: Mother's Father,
My Grandfather Yitzchak Abramson
Sitting: Betty and Leon Rothenberg
Esther and Myer Tulkoff
Tulkoff Wedding, March 7, 1953

© 2018. All Rights Reserved. Esther Tulkoff, I'M ALIVE HURRAY

I'M ALIVE HURRAY

Bottom: Esther, Myer, and Daisy Tulkoff
Middle: Ruth and Sol Rothenberg
Back Left: Reva'a Son Baruch

Beloved Family Photos

Daisy Chihuahua Tulkoff Drives a Buick

© 2018. All Rights Reserved. Esther Tulkoff, I'M ALIVE HURRAY

I'M ALIVE HURRAY

Colonel Myer S. Tulkoff Dedication Bench Plaque Century Village East, Florida

© 2018. All Rights Reserved. Esther Tulkoff, I'M ALIVE HURRAY

Beloved Family Photos

Esther Tulkoff
"HURRAY I'M ALIVE" T-shirt (first draft)
"I'M ALIVE HURRAY" (final draft and title)
Colonel Myer Tulkoff Dedication Bench
Century Village East, Florida
June 2018

© 2018. All Rights Reserved. Esther Tulkoff, I'M ALIVE HURRAY

I'M ALIVE HURRAY

Beloved Family Letters

I'M ALIVE HURRAY

Rabbi Nachum Muschel, 2006

Beloved Family Letters

Rabbi Nachum Muschel, 2006

December 5, 2006

Dear Esther and Myer:

Apparently you didn't do a very good job of hiding in a cloud of anonymity, and you were discovered in Deerfield Beach, Florida.

For the Young Israel of Deerfield Beach, it is a discovery. For us, in Monsey, it's merely a reiteration of what we know about the Tulkoffs. Clearly, there is much more than your community in Deerfield Beach found out by now.

To us, you remain the Tulkoffs of Monsey who raised their family here, who joined a community endeavor in spreading Torah education, and who participated in every worthy action that strengthens the Jewish people. At ASHAR, the Tulkoff's name is written indelibly on the hearts of young children who carried out of these halls the inspiration and curiosity that fill them with love of Torah and with eagerness to do Mitzvot. As they sang their songs, prepared their projects, and offered little plays for hundreds of parents over the years, Esther became the crowned queen of our early childhood education.

Time does not erase these achievements. These feelings are transformed into respect, affection and friendship that we bring to you at this time when you ready yourselves to allow others to put a spotlight on you.

Let the light shine and let the world know that you have the commitment, the devotion, and affection that builds Jewish continuity.

Congratulations on your forthcoming honor. Keep doing things that remind us to continue to be proud of you and all of yours.

Finally yours,
Rabbi N. Muschel

I'M ALIVE HURRAY

Aide Ann Marie Treasure

5/9/16 3:51 P.M.

Esther
The love + commitment you had for your late husband, I love that you love your children & still worry about them, I love the way you light up when you talk about your grand children and great grandchildren, I love your amazing sense of humor. I love that even though there's a difference in our age, race, religion and nationality you didn't let it divide us you've had such an impact on my life. I love you, have a happy Mother's Day
~~love~~ Anne Marie

Beloved Family Letters

Joe DiMaggio Children's Hospital Foundation $1000 Donation

March 15, 2016

Mrs. Esther Tulkoff
1 Ashbury A
Deerfield Beach, FL 33442

Dear Mrs. Tulkoff:

On behalf of the patients served by Memorial Healthcare System, thank you for your gift dated March 26, 2016 in the amount of $1,000 in honor of Dr. Jeromy Jacobs, Ximena Tapia and Trenton Barrick as Memorial Angels. We have designated your gift to the Memorial Regional South Fund, which will provide exceptional quality healthcare to countless people in our community.

Thanks to you and all the people in our community who care about world-class healthcare, we are able to save lives... because we believe that everyone who comes through our doors deserves access to the best advanced care and treatment available.

Please know that your Memorial Angels will receive notification announcing that you have made a donation in their honor, with no mention of the amount, as well as a custom-crafted lapel pin for them to wear proudly.

Again, on behalf of the people in our community who will benefit from your generous contribution, I sincerely and deeply thank you.

Sincerely,

Thank you very much!

Kevin R. Janser
Senior Vice President and Chief Development Officer
Memorial Healthcare System

IN CONFORMITY WITH IRS GUIDELINES, PLEASE BE ADVISED THAT, UNLESS OTHERWISE STATED, WE HAVE NOT PROVIDED YOU WITH ANY GOODS OR SERVICES IN CONSIDERATION OF THIS CONTRIBUTION. PLEASE SAVE THIS GIFT ACKNOWLEDGMENT FOR YOUR TAX RETURN. A COPY OF THE OFFICIAL REGISTRATION AND FINANCIAL INFORMATION FOR MEMORIAL FOUNDATION (CH-04059) MAY BE OBTAINED FROM THE DIVISION OF CONSUMER SERVICES BY CALLING TOLL-FREE 1-800-435-7352 WITHIN THE STATE. REGISTRATION DOES NOT IMPLY ENDORSEMENT, APPROVAL, OR RECOMMENDATION BY THE STATE.

MEMORIAL REGIONAL HOSPITAL • MEMORIAL REGIONAL HOSPITAL SOUTH • JOE DIMAGGIO CHILDREN'S HOSPITAL
MEMORIAL HOSPITAL WEST • MEMORIAL HOSPITAL MIRAMAR • MEMORIAL HOSPITAL PEMBROKE • MEMORIAL MANOR

3711 Garfield Street • Hollywood, FL 33021 • (954) 265-3454 • Fax: (954) 966-6750
www.mhsfoundation.org • www.jdchf.org

Remember us in your estate plan today - and help create a healthier future

© 2018. All Rights Reserved. Esther Tulkoff, I'M ALIVE HURRAY

I'M ALIVE HURRAY

Young Israel of Deerfield Beach and Israel Bonds

Our Honorees

Col. Myer and Esther Tulkoff are active members of the Young Israel of Deerfield Beach and Hebrew Institute of White Plains, New York. His father, Robert Tulkoff A"H, was the mainstay of the little one-room shul, serving as Chazzan, shamus and Baal Koreh in the small town of Ashland, Kentucky—where Myer was born and raised. Esther was born in Louisville, Kentucky, where her father, Rabbi Leon Rothenberg, a Telzundic Scholar, was Rabbi and Schochet and later moved to Baltimore, where Myer and Esther met.

Esther attended the University of Maryland and graduated from Eastern College of Commerce in Baltimore and Bais Yaakov Teacher's Seminary in New York, later specializing in Early Childhood Education. She taught kindergarten for 30 years.

The military has been a major interest in Myer's life. He served in Japan and Korea and in the active army reserve until he retired with the rank of Colonel. He graduated from the University Of Kentucky College Of Law where he made law review and graduated with honors. He is a member of the Kentucky and New York bars. Myer was Assistant Regional Director of the New York field Office of the Federal Trade Commission. He supervised the investigation and prosecution of consumer fraud, false advertising cases and other violations of federal laws and antitrust matters. After retiring from the FTC, he worked for AT&T in its antitrust legal department. He frequently conducted lectures at seminars.

Their daughter Donna resides in Great Neck, NY with her husband Dr. Leon Schwechter, son Cary and daughter Serena who is currently studying in Israel for one year. Their oldest son Daniel, his wife Yael and daughter Shira Malka reside in Queens. Daniel is graduating Y.U. Smicha program and is the Rabbi and intern in training, at Great Neck Synagogue.

Their son Jonathan, CEO of Unawire Int'l and wife Lynette, a commercial real estate broker, and daughters Sophie and Olivia, reside in New Rochelle, New York.

Young Israel of Deerfield Beach
&
State of Israel Bonds

cordially invite you to a

Breakfast

honoring

Esther and Myer Tulkoff

Sunday, February 13, 2011 at 9:45 a.m.

Guest Speaker
Brigadier General (Ret) Yehuda Halevy

Young Israel of Deerfield Beach
202 Century Boulevard
Deerfield Beach

Reservations required
Couvert $8.00 per person

Dietary laws observed

To purchase tickets please call Young Israel of Deerfield Beach
(954) 571 3904

All are welcome

© 2018. All Rights Reserved. Esther Tulkoff, I'M ALIVE HURRAY

Beloved Family Letters

Young Israel of Deerfield Beach and Israel Bonds

ESTHER AND MYER TULKOFF

Young Israel of Deerfield Beach recently honored Esther and Myer Tulkoff at its 27th anniversary dinner in February. The Tulkoffs received a Kesser Shem Tov (Crown of a Good Name Award) for their dedication and commitment to the synagogue. Both are originally from Kentucky, and have served Jewish communities throughout the country. Myer has co-chaired the Israel Bond Breakfast of Young Israel for several years and he is the videographer for all major functions. This year, Esther chaired the sisterhood's Purim program.

© 2018. All Rights Reserved. Esther Tulkoff, I'M ALIVE HURRAY

I'M ALIVE HURRAY

Beauty School License
1981

```
                STATE OF NEW JERSEY
          DEPARTMENT OF LAW AND PUBLIC SAFETY
              DIVISION OF CONSUMER AFFAIRS
PASTE
                    THIS IS TO CERTIFY THAT
PHOTO         BOARD OF BEAUTY CULTURE
HERE                   HAS LICENSED

               ESTHER          TULKOFF
               118 W MAPLE AVE
               MONSEY                    NY
                                         10952
   FOR PRACTICE IN NEW JERSEY AS A(N)  OPERATOR

     10/01/81          09/30/83            WE35201
    EFFECTIVE DATE    EXPIRATION DATE     LICENSE NO.

   SIGNATURE OF REGISTRANT               DIRECTOR
```

© 2018. All Rights Reserved. Esther Tulkoff, I'M ALIVE HURRAY

Beloved Family Letters

Beauty School License
1983

```
                    STATE OF NEW JERSEY
              DEPARTMENT OF LAW AND PUBLIC SAFETY
                  DIVISION OF CONSUMER AFFAIRS
   PASTE
                      THIS IS TO CERTIFY THAT
   PHOTO          BOARD OF BEAUTY CULTURE
   HERE                   HAS LICENSED


                  ESTHER          TULKOFF
                  118 W MAPLE AVE
                  MONSEY                  NY
                                       10952
   FOR PRACTICE IN NEW JERSEY AS A(N)  OPERATOR

      10/01/83           09/30/85           WE35201
     EFFECTIVE DATE     EXPIRATION DATE     LICENSE NO.

     SIGNATURE OF REGISTRANT                DIRECTOR
```

© 2018. All Rights Reserved. Esther Tulkoff, I'M ALIVE HURRAY

I'M ALIVE HURRAY

For Literary Manuscript Collectors and Curators

Original Handwritten Manuscript of Authoritis* Esther Tulkoff

*Excruciatingly Painful Arthritis

Jonathan

Jonathan 6/27/18

Jonathan was born when Donna was 6 yrs old.

When we did not have another child in 5 years, I went to a gynacologist Doctor, and after an exam, he told me that I was what they call a "one child sterility case." I was upset, but I told myself that I have to thank G-d that I had such a beautiful daughter and I should thank G-d for what I considered the biggest blessing in the world. After a few weeks of kind of adjusting to this, I finally decided to give her carriage and stroller to charity. That was when I became pregnant with Jonathan. My H & I were soo delighted to add a son to our family. We felt we should name him Jonathan — which comes from the Hebrew Words "Hashem Natan" (Hashem Has Given). We had to buy new baby necessities. We felt soo LUCKY!

*Sharon - please add this to this page
LUVU
Esther

I'M ALIVE HURRAY

When children are young, their parents talk about how smart they are; When parents are old, their children talk about how stupid they are.

Ven di kinder zaynen yung
dertseyln di eltern zeyere khokhmes;
ven di eltern zaynen alt
dertseyln di kinder zeyere narishkaytn.

Yiddish Classic, Unknown

I'M ALIVE HURRAY

Retirement

Who Died Today?

June 2018: Every morning, these past ten days, another call from Young Israel of Deerfield Beach, "I'm sorry to announce that one of our members has passed away and the funeral will be at (address) and (time) and Shiva will be observed at (address) and (time). May Hashem comfort them among the mourners of Zion and Jerusalem."

Not only is that sad, but its kind of scary.

I guess I should say thanks Hashem that it is not my turn today. Every night, I say a prayer and its called Kreat Shema thanking Hashem for his care of me and thanking him and asking him for his blessings to each and every member of the family.

I include a blessing for Ian, brother of Lynette Luyt Tulkoff and son of Jean Luyt. I hope my prayers are heard and acted on by Hashem.

I'M ALIVE HURRAY

Suffering is always hard to quantify – especially when the pain is caused by as cruel a disease as Alzheimer's. Most illnesses attack the body; Alzheimer's destroys the mind – and in the process, annihilates the very self.

Jeffrey Kluger

I'M ALIVE HURRAY

Alzheimers

Hey Kids: Myer and Mary

All good, until Myer got Alzheimer's for four and a half years. The first year I covered for him. The second and third year, I hired an aide to help wake, wash, and dress him.

I was so stressed out when Myer's aide Pedro quit on a Friday night and said he had another full time job. And Pedro had to be there on Sunday. I told him, "That is not nice!" But I could do nothing about it. I made many calls, but could not find an aide to come when I needed him. I needed the aide to come early morning to help get Myer ready to go to Alzheimer's day care, and be here when Myer came back in the afternoon.

I had to pay out-of-pocket for the aide, for two years to come in the morning, to help get Myer ready to go to Alzheimer's day care. The aide came back in the

I'M ALIVE HURRAY

afternoon to help ready him for the evening. I paid him $20 an hour. He was there for four hours a day. $400 dollars a week. That came out to a lot of money.

I could not get a new aide for Myer to replace Pedro, so I had to find a nursing home for him that had an Alzheimer's care section.

The Veteran's Administration did not help us. I did everything to try to get financial help.

Finally, I was able to get him into a nursing home with an Alzheimer's care section. It was about a five to ten minute drive. I paid three thousand dollars a month and went everyday, at different times, twice or three times a day. Everyday at different times, so the aides did not know when I was coming. This I felt kept them on their toes. Those nursing home aides were below par as far as I was concerned!

I noticed a sweet lady who had no visitors and I asked her if she had a visitor today. She said she never had visitors, so I invited her to come everyday to join Myer and me. She was so happy.

I would prepare jokes and stories for Myer and for Mary, the lady who never had visitors, and she looked forward to my visit as well. I greeted them both with,
"Hey kids, I have a great DVD for you!"
They really enjoyed my gifts of entertainment.
I would sit with them, watch a movie on a screen in the main room, or take them to his room and listen to tapes.

He was actually doing as well as could be expected.

I'M ALIVE HURRAY

I Love You Too!

Once when Donna came from New York to visit her father in the home:

Donna said, "Hi daddy, I'm your daughter Donna. I love you."

He said, "I love you too!"

She walked around the room, came back, and said, "What's my name daddy?"

He could not remember. She went to the corner and cried.

My son Jonathan came quite often also, and was heartbroken. They both adored their father. I tried my best to look happy and make him happy.

I'M ALIVE HURRAY

The New England Journal of Medicine reports that 9 out of 10 doctors agree that 1 out of 10 doctors is an idiot.

Jay Leno

I'M ALIVE HURRAY

*Dr. Drek**

I experienced such a horrible pain in my neck and shoulders that I thought I ate poison. I didn't even remember what I ate. Maybe it was something spoiled in the refrigerator.

    I was waiting for the rain to stop so I could go to the Alzheimer's home, as I did every day for two years. I would cut Myer's nails when necessary, shave him when he needed, take Kosher food to him, and make sure he was clean. I would then spend quite a bit of time to entertain or keep him happy in some way.
I did this everyday for two years, until that Saturday when they took me to the hospital.

    A few weeks before I went to the hospital, Myer had fallen at the home, and they did not call me until after he was taken to what I considered to be the worst hospital in the area.

I'M ALIVE HURRAY

I rushed over and went to his room. The doctor was talking to Myer.

I said, "Dr. Ameer. I am his wife. He has Alzheimers. I think you should talk to me."

He said, "He is my patient. You are not my patient."

"But doctor, I said, he doesn't understand. I have to understand what you're saying."

He said, "If you don't like it, get another doctor."

Another doctor walked by and I called him in and dismissed Dr. Ameer, and reported him to the head nurse. Dr. Drek caused Myer to stay another two days. I was livid. I tried to do all I could to have him fired from the hospital. I never heard anything happened and believe it or not, he sent me a bill from his office.

I called the office and said,

"If I ever hear from him again, my lawyer will sue him." I never heard from Dr. Drek* again.

*Drek is Yiddish for S-H-I-T! (or garbage)

I'm Going to Jail

A few days before, I made a last attempt to get financial help for my husband in the Alzheimer's nursing home. The VA would not help us in any way financially, when he was stricken with Alzheimers. I wrote letters. I went to their offices and tried to contact people at the VA, to no avail. The VA caused me much stress.

I was told by a friend to drive to the Sunrise Veteran's Administration. A man named Juan would help me get financial help for my husband the retired colonel who served his country for thirty years and who now has Alzheimers. He was wounded in Japan, but did not report it.

I had been to many VA offices. The service was generally horrendous. They said he was not entitled

I'M ALIVE HURRAY

to financial help. So I was going to try once again to get financial assistance for his Alzheimer's disease.

The friend advised me to go to Sunrise VA and ask for Juan, "I really think he will help you." Just before I left, Roz Noble called and asked if I was going out? She does not drive, and asked if she could go with me for a drive. So we got there and waited for about a half hour. I was terribly upset. A little fat lady came out to the waiting room and said,

"Who's next?"

I raised my hand, and said,

"I am, but I am waiting for Juan.

She said, "He is not here today."

So I said, "So."

She loudly exclaimed, "You come with me!"

I knew I was in trouble already. So I said to Roz, who was waiting with me,

"Stay here, I'll be right back."

So I walked into her office with her.

The first thing she said was, "Well, I need this paper, and this paper, and this paper!"

I said, "Madame, I sent into your agency at least three copies, three times, where are they?"

She said, "Well I ain't got them."

So I said, "I ain't got them either!" And I stormed out.

We got into my car.

Roz said,"What happened?"

I said, "Nothing!"

I asked, "What day is today?"

Roz said, "Tuesday."

I said, "Uh Oh! were lost. We may not get home till after the Sabbath."

Just then, I saw a road I recognized and turned onto it. We heard a siren. I stopped the car and a cop came over to me.

I said, "Did you stop me?"

He said, "Yes!"

I said, "For what?"

He said, "Speeding!"

I said, "Look at me officer, I have been driving since I was fifteen years old and I never got a speeding ticket. Do you think I started today? I'm going to ask you

I'M ALIVE HURRAY

very nicely, please do not give me a ticket! My plate is full! My husband is a retired full colonel and has had Alzheimer's disease for four and a half years. He served in the army in Japan, Korea, and twenty-eight years in the Military Government, second in command of 600 troops. The U.S. Government and the Veteran's Administration is making me sick. I'm going to ask you once again. Please do not give me a ticket."

The cop said, "If you don't give me your license and your registration, I am going to take you to jail."

I said, "That is the best offer I have had all day. I'm going to your jail to rest, and you go and take care of my retired full colonel."

Roz sitting next to me almost had a heart attack. She thought she would have to go to jail with me, I think.

The officer looked and looked at me. I guess he was thinking what to do, I also was thinking, what is he going to say when he brings me to jail?

He said to me after a few minutes,

"Get out of here!"

I almost didn't go.

Roz said, "Get out of here, we can go!"

I said to Roz,

"Could you imagine what he told his wife when he went home. Some little old lady wanted to go to jail to rest and said, I should take care of her husband the Full Colonel who has Alzheimers."

I'M ALIVE HURRAY

Myer's Birthday Cupcakes & 15 Stitches

For Myer's birthday, on Thursday, October 24th, I was going to make him a party at the nursing home. I bought twenty-four large cupcakes and two birthday cakes.

My cousins, Toby and Joel Bofshaver, who came quite often were there.

I rushed into the home and fell in the hall. I cracked my forehead. The cupcakes and cakes fell out of my hands and I started to bleed very badly. The cakes stayed in their bags. I told the aides to put the cakes in the fridge and we would have the party on Sunday.

Toby and Joel took me to the hospital. I had fifteen stitches put over my eyebrows. They drove me back to the home to get my car, and I went in to say that I was not going to sue, so that I would not endanger care for Myer.

I'M ALIVE HURRAY

I have to say, I appreciated when people came to visit with me and Myer. Roz Noble came with me often. My kids were coming back and forth from New York to visit with him and to keep my spirits up.

We did have the party on Sunday. And Miriam and Abe Tous came. We have been best friends since we both got married. Myer taught Abe how to drive. This was Myer's last birthday party.

I'M ALIVE HURRAY

The Angel of Death Knocks on Two Doors Bubbe and Grandpa

(How Come I'm Bubbe and Your Grandpa?)

One Finger Miracle Alert

Just about 2 weeks before I had a terrible pain, and had to use my life alert on a Saturday which incidentally was within reach of my hand by some miracle. I walked from the dining room table to the living room couch, and I was only able to move one finger to press my alert system. I could not have pressed 911.

They answered and asked if this was Esther Tulkoff. I said, "Yes!"

He said, "Are you alright?"

I said, "No, I think I am having a stroke."

He said, "Don't eat anything and don't get up. The ambulance is on its way."

A young man came in when the ambulance arrived.

I said, "Young man, I am not going into your ambulance if you don't take me to Boca Regional Hospital."

I'M ALIVE HURRAY

Second young man came in and I said to him,

"Young man, did you hear what I told the other young man?"

He said, "Yes Ma'am."

Then we all heard the driver in the ambulance yell out,

"Lady, get into the ambulance! I'm going to take you to Boca Regional."

They usually take Century Village East residents to Broward North Hospital. A few weeks prior to this, Myer was taken to Broward North Hospital after a fall in the home, and they could not reach me. I had to deal with Dr. Drek.*

(*Yiddish: S-H-I-T or garbage)

I'M ALIVE HURRAY

Do as much as possible for the patient, and little as possible to the patient.

Dr. Bernard Lown

I'M ALIVE HURRAY

Misdiagnosis, Fistfight, Finger Nerve Endings, Neck Neurosurgery, and Myer Goes to Hospice
December 1, 2015

It was a miracle that I was able to reach my medical alert button and an ambulance took me to the hospital.

You must always have an advocate when you go to a doctor or to the hospital. I was taken to Boca Regional Hospital. The nurses, or a doctor I did not know put two needles into my arms. My whole arms turned black and blue almost up to the shoulder. It looked awful. To this day, my fingers do not work properly.

That was one week before Dr. Schwechter came to my hospital room and a neurosurgeon was there.

(Dr. Putz) The neurosurgeon said, "Her husband may die Saturday or Sunday, so we will do surgery for a stroke on Monday.

(Dr. Mensch) Dr. Schwechter from New York said, "I don't agree that she had a stroke!"

I'M ALIVE HURRAY

(**Dr. Putz**) The neurosurgeon got up and tried to hit Dr. Schwechter.

Dr. Putz: "I am the neurosurgeon and I say its a stroke." Doctors, nurses, and aides heard what was happening and they came into my room.

(**Dr. Mensch**) My doctor replied:

"I am a doctor from New York, and we as a family dismiss you and we will decide what to do."

My doctor sent a letter to the hospital informing them of the neurosurgeon's flagrant misdiagnosis and threatened a fistfight, and **Dr. Putz** was fired.

All **Dr. Putz** he had to do was take an X-RAY and he would have seen that a disc from my neck fell onto my spine.

My N.Y. doctor called up his neurosurgeon who said, that I must have spinal surgery in the morning. To this day, I have seven nails and bolts in my neck and am doing well thanks to Dr. Leon Schwechter and G-d.

I was misdiagnosed as having a stroke which I did not have. When I asked a nurse what a stroke, surgery would have done, I was told that I probably would have been a quadriplegic for the rest of my life!

After two years in a nursing home for Alzheimers, my husband Myer was sent to a hospice exactly one week after I was taken to the hospital. To me that meant he was not getting the care he needed.

I could not go every day like I did for two years once twice or three times a day to cut his nails when needed, shave him, and take Kosher food to him, and to make sure he was clean.

I just knew those nursing homes aides were not great. One reason I went so much, I knew that he would not get the right care if I was not there. Many of those aides were lazy, fat, and nasty.

Rabbi Edelman of Young Israel of Deerfield Beach has a special place in my heart as does his Rebbetzin Gutel for their support and comforting that they were to me. I will never forget how he and his wife came to visit me at the hospital. They were told to go to the occupational therapy room to find me. When he walked in, I was beating a drum for therapy. I told the therapist that my Rabbi just walked in. He invited the Rabbi to join us and gave him a drum. I will always remember what a good sport he is, as he joined me to beat a drum.

I'M ALIVE HURRAY

I Will Always Love You

Ten days after major surgery which was on December 1, 2015, my doctor, Jeremy Jacobs came into my hospital room and asked me if I would like to go out. I could barely sit up myself much less go out.

I said, "You will let me out of this jail?"

He said, "No, I will just give you a day out."

I said, "I will take it!"

He arranged for my physical therapist Ximena to help me. She practically carried me with a neck brace and all else to Lenore Eisenberg's car to drive me to Myer in hospice. Nearby aides also assisted.

Also, Trenton Barrick was wonderful to me as the occupational therapist. Incidentally, I will never forget how the Eisenberg family was there for me so much. I love you guys.

I'M ALIVE HURRAY

Donna met us there and wheeled me into Myer's room at the hospice. He looked awful. Donna left me with him alone. We had a way of letting each other know that he knew who I was, and I knew who he was, and I knew that he knew I was there.

I told Myer, "I love you very much and I am so sorry I am so sick. As soon as I am well, I will take care of you as I always have. Look at all the NACHES* we have! (*Yiddish:pride).

Billy Eisenberg still remembers how Dr. Schwecter called him when he was visiting me at the hospital, and asked him to see if I could button his shirt to test my flexibility. I tried and tried but could not do it.

Finally, I said, "I can't button you up, but I can unzip your pants." We both started to laugh.

He said, "You know I'm married!"

My beloved children, Donna and Jonathan both commented on the TZURIS* (*Yiddish: problems) of having both of their parents in the hospital at the same time. The fear of possibly losing two parents simultaneously and planning for two funerals was intense.

Donna came in and said,

"I have to take you back to the hospital."

I told Myer, "I will always love you." He died at 3 A.M. that night.

Myer was such a good person and helped many people pro bono in his law practice. He received many awards for pro bono work. I was very proud of him. I did think we could have been much richer, but not as happy!

I remember one very funny story. A black man called, I forgot his name but he was a very nice man. When he came to Myer, to ask for legal help, Myer asked him how he knew to call Myer. He said, I looked in the telephone book for a Jewish lawyer, because I know they are smart and good. Myer met with him a few times and he was very happy. He started to call Myer on the phone after a week or two and he could not say Myer's last name. So when he called, he would say, "Is Mr. Tuchus* there?" (*Tuchus is Yiddish: anatomy behind, butt, ass).

I'M ALIVE HURRAY

I would yell up to Myer very loud...

"Mr. Tuchus, there's a call for you!" I did this about three times and Myer said after the third call,

"Don't call me, Mr. Tuchus anymore or else!"

I didn't do it after that, but it was funny, even he laughed.

Five days after I had major neck surgery, I could not breathe. I said to myself,

"Son of a gun, I am not going to die before I get every penny the Veteran's Administration owes me!"

It was the middle of the night. No doctors were there. No nurses came in and no aides were around. So saying I'm not going to die, mean't that I had to figure out how to catch my breath. What I did, I closed half of my lips so I could pull harder that air that I needed into my lungs. And it worked. And I could finally breathe.

I said, "Thank you, Hashem*" (*Yiddish for G-D).

I called Lynette, Jonathan's wife from the hospital crying.

I said, "I am so sad that I am not as beautiful as you, not as smart, and as wonderful a cook as you are, and will not be remembered very well when I die."

She assured me that I was not going to die, and I would be remembered with lots of love and everything.

I'M ALIVE HURRAY

Missed Myer's Funeral
December 10, 2015

After Myer died, and the funeral I could not go, so my children streamed the funeral to the hospital where we had to move from my room to an auditorium because close to 40 people came to be with me. I was very touched by the love shown to me during Shiva.*
(*Yiddish: mourning period)

    Rabbi Lewis and Melissa Weineker, Daniel's wife's parents came to make a Shiva call from N.Y. They came and went back that day. I was so touched. I needed one hundred dollars to pay the aide, so I reluctantly asked if they could loan me the money. Without a thought, he took out a hundred dollars.

I'M ALIVE HURRAY

What a wonderful couple they are. But I must say, it did bother me, so I asked Donna to pay them back and she did.

Another surprise visit, among many during Shiva,* was Michelle and Herbie Mossberg (Leon's sister and brother-in-law) came to see me in the hospital. I was delighted to see them. I must admit that I always had a special feeling for Herbie.

A kindergarten graduate of mine, David Noble, who now has a married daughter, made a Shiva* call to me. I was delighted to see him.

After the funeral that I could not go to, I was also unable to leave the hospital to sit Shiva.* So many people came to the hospital to pay a Shiva* visit. I was in the hospital a month and a half. After many months, I was able to go to Myer's grave.

It is hard to believe that after 62 years of marriage to this great guy, I was unable to go to his funeral and to sit Shiva* in our home. It was the most horrible and depressing feeling, in addition to losing my husband. I miss Myer very much.

I'M ALIVE HURRAY

We may encounter many defeats, but we must not be defeated.

Maya Angelou

I'M ALIVE HURRAY

The Angel of Death Won't Let Go of Me!

Dr. Gonif: What Did You Do? My Bubblegum Tooth Horror Story

I must try to warn people not to go to him. One Friday evening, I pulled a tooth out with gum. But I knew it could be glued back in.

I went to Dr. G. after being advised that he was a very good dentist by a neighbor. Thanks Beth for telling me to go to him.

She said, "Why should you drive so far to your other dentist?"

Office Visit 1. On Monday, I went to Dr. G. and asked him to glue it in. He did not want to do it. I was ready to leave. He said, "Alright." And I thought he glued it in. It fell out the next day. So I went back to his office.

Office Visit 2. What he said exactly is...

"Go into the next room and we will fix it!"
I was still recovering from serious neck surgery and he could see that I was not well. It was obvious.

I'M ALIVE HURRAY

I thought, it was just going to be glued in. His partner asked me to sit and he would fix it, not what he would fix. Before I knew, the dentist cut my gums on the other side very quickly and before I knew what he was doing, I almost fainted! I was in shock. I cried,

"What did you do?

He said, "You need that done!"

I had no problem or pain on that side of my mouth. I said, "Are you nuts?"

I would have stopped him if I saw what he was doing. I'm sure that in dental school the first thing they learn is a diabetic must take antibiotics before any mouth surgery. I am diabetic and must take antibiotics before any surgery in my mouth. Every dentist knows that and should ask, "Are you diabetic?"

He said, "Come back next week."

I did not know what to do.

Office visit 3. I went back a week later to see what he would do. He just said, "It is not healed yet!" I knew that I would never go back into that office again, He opened up a can of worms, to make sure that he could make money from what he did to my mouth.

What was happening, an infection from mymouth was moving towards my brain. I knew something was wrong, I did not feel right.

Dr. Schmucks: I went to two other dentists who did not want to get involved. One was a dentist I had been going to for many years. I will never use him again, nor will I ever send anyone I know to him for any dental service.

The next week, I went back to the dentist that cut my gums and did not prescribe antibiotics. The office girl I call her, "Piss-mouth" tried to give me a bill. I stormed out and went to Dr. Gregory who said, "Mrs Tulkoff, you are very sick." He gave me a prescription for antibiotics and said, "You must start immediately and take all." The infection was headed up to my brain and he would not charge me. I think he saved my life. He saved my life from the can of worms that Dr. Gonif* created.

When I got home, I called the dental association.

I said, "I would like to report a dentist in Century Village East."

She said, Are you talking about Dr. Gonif*?"

I said, "Yes."

I'M ALIVE HURRAY

She said, "Well I have ten complaints on my desk now!"

I said, "Tomorrow, you will have eleven!"

That week, I received a credit card bill for $4000 from Wells Fargo. I was livid. He took out a credit card in my name without my knowledge. I called Wells Fargo and sent a letter to the Florida Attorney General. A case was opened and the money was returned. How upsetting that was. I called my dental insurance to not pay his office anything.

They said they could not, without an X-ray of my entire mouth. I was relieved and that was over.

He never took an X-ray of my mouth, but he sent an X-ray of someone else because I never had an X-ray taken there. He must have because they paid him.

I can't believe that what should have been a simple visit to a dentist to glue in a tooth escalated into a fraudulent case of malpractice that almost caused my death by infection.

And even though I was still recovering from the major neck surgery in Boca Regional Hospital, because a disc from my neck fell onto my spine, I now had a new medical problem caused by Dr. Gonif.* I was very distressed.

I still had an aide 24/7, for four and a half months after my neck surgery.

Karen my substitute aide, a big strong girl went to the office of the dentist with me to get copies of my dental records. His nasty office girl, we called her, "Ms. Piss-mouth," would not give us the dental records, and said, I would have to pay to get a copy of my dental records.

Karen said, she was going back to knock out all of Ms. Piss-mouth's teeth and knock the doctor's head off.

I said, "Karen, please don't. I said, I am too sick to help you in Jail." I was too sick to continue to work with the Florida Attorney General, and try to to have him charged with fraud and to sue him.

And three days later, I was in the hospital fighting another life-threatening disease: THE BIG ONE!

* Gonif is Yiddish for a disreputable or dishonest person

I'M ALIVE HURRAY

Dr. Mensch: Dr. Leon Schwechter He came to my rescue after every medical episode of misdiagnosis, mistreatment, and malpractice. He is my hero.

Dr. Drek: Refused to talk to me. He only wanted to talk to Myer, an Alzheimer's patient who did not understand him. Dr. Drek told me to get another doctor, and I took his excellent advice!

Dr. Putz: Misdiagnosis of a stroke and starting a fistfight with Dr. Mensch. Dr. Putz was fired. Needles were placed in my arms and my fingers have never recovered - mistreatment and malpractice.

Dr. Pisher: Misdiagnosis, mistreatment, and malpractice- pumping my stomach for three weeks without an x-ray.

Dr. Gonif: Unnecessary dental surgery on wrong side of my mouth and I'm a diabetic. I filed a complaint, number eleven, with the dental association.

Dr. Schmuck(s): Refused to provide emergency medical treatment for Dr. Gonif's dental infection. After years of dental treatment as his patient, he did not want to get involved!

Every patient's greatest fear is that the doctor is going to kill you before the disease.

Sharon Esther Lampert
Poet, Philosopher, Peacemaker, Prophet

I'M ALIVE HURRAY

Primum non nocere
                        first, to do no harm

1st Leading Cause of Death - Heart Attacks

2nd Leading Cause of Death - Cancer

3rd Leading Cause of Death
Estimated deaths from medical errors
210,00-440,000

Source: Journal of Patient Safety, 2018

3 Weeks of Malpractice Medical Treatment Before Diagnosis

I had been out of the hospital after neck surgery for three weeks. Ann Marie, my wonderful aide was still with me and she was going to go back to New York the same time as I was going to spend Passover with my family.

Dr.s Mensch: I appreciated the care I received and made a donation to the Joe DiMaggio Children's Hospital Foundation of $1000 in honor of the three caregivers: Dr. Jeremy Jacobs, Ximena Tapia, and Trenton Barrick (see "Beloved Letters").

I was called to attend a special program to honor the three special people who did so much to help me to begin recovery. I was so touched. I was supposed to be called up to the stage, as a surprise for them, and was excited about about seeing them. However, I got sick again about a few weeks before the program. I missed the event.

I'M ALIVE HURRAY

Dr. Pisher: I went to the hospital three times in three weeks for an undiagnosed pain in my stomach. The symptoms were vomiting, pain, and the inability to move my bowels. The hospital nurses each time put a straw through the nose to my stomach to clean it out. Each week, I was sent home and had to come back the following week, until the third time.

I exclaimed, " You better find out what's wrong with me!"

Five Hours of Poison Injections

However, I got so sick again about a week before the celebration at the Orlando-Passover holiday. I had a blockage in my stomach and had surgery to remove it that day. I was not told right away that it was lymphoma cancer.

Because it was just before Passover, my kids did not want to upset me before I came to Orlando, Florida to celebrate Passover together. I really did not feel great, but I was happy to be with my children, grandchildren, and great grandchildren.

After being there, a few days, I was told I had to go to New York for chemotherapy. It was something I would not wish on anyone.

I was sitting in a room with five-seven other chemotherapy patients getting poison injected into our arms for five hours. We kind of got to know each other and I really tried to make it easier to stand up to it. Two other teachers were my buddies. I started telling funny kindergarten stories that would make us laugh.

I'M ALIVE HURRAY

I told how I had to call a mother in the second day of school and say to her, "We have a problem! I am a teacher and not a psychologist."

She said, "We don't have a problem. You have a problem!"

I said, "Oh No! We have a problem!"

She almost got nasty and said, "My son has been in three nurseries, and I never got a call from them."

I said, "I would like to call and speak with them because they did not do their job."

"Oh No!" She said, "That is not necessary!"

I got Dr. David Koplon, the school psychologist to work with us. At the end of the school year, I received a beautiful letter thanking me for doing such a great job in developing her son so well. I followed him up to the fourth grade, and he was doing very well. I was very happy.

After chemotherapy, my hair fell out and I wore a lovely wig for a few months. One day, as I was visiting with my daughter, the wig fell off as I made a fast move and my daughter said,

"Mom your hair is beautiful. You don't have to wear the wig anymore!"

And I do have to say, that my hair grew in beautifully in white. I like it till today.

Until I was in my later thirties, I had to die my hair black every month or so to cover the grey. I kept saying to Myer, that I wanted to dye my hair blonde. Would he be upset? He said, "Do it if you want to." And every once in a while, he would ask why it wasn't blonde yet? Finally, one day I went to the salon, and they stripped the hair twice and colored it blonde. I felt like I looked like little orphan Annie. And that evening, there was a program for parents at my school and I thought I better be seen by parents before I went back to school. I called my kindergarten assistant, Ahuva, to please come to school with me in the evening so I could walk in and not be alone.

Rabbi Chanofsky was addressing the audience. I had been teaching kindergarten in the school for fifteen years, as a dark-haired lady. When I opened the door, there was a sudden gasp of all of the parents when they

I'M ALIVE HURRAY

saw me. Rabbi Chanofsky said, using a microphone,

"What just happened?"

So I waived at everybody and we left. The next morning when I came to school I did not say,

"Boker tov or good morning."

I just said, "Do you like it?"

And most kids were almost speechless, not afraid but were almost concerned. One little boy raised his hand and said to me,

"I would love you with black hair or white hair."

I said, "Honey, you are going right to the second grade."

I got a call the next day from a mother and she said her son came home and said,

"We have to behave better in kindergarten because Morah* Tulkoff's hair turned white overnight." It was really funny!

*Morah is Hebrew for teacher

I'm So Disgusted, I Can't Even Talk About It!
June 2018

The latest obstacle that I am trying to overcome with levity is that I have had to go for squamish cancer surgery on my leg in two places.

Many seniors in Florida develop skin cancer on the face. My skin cancer appreared on my leg and was removed. It reappeared on the same leg again and I'm so disgusted! The medical procedure is called Mohs surgery. A piece of skin for each cancer was taken from the back of my neck and stitched to the top of my two wounds.

I advise everyone to always check their medical problem with another doctor.

So I went to my internist Dr. Weissman. He checked and ordered a home nurse to come every day to dress the wounds. I really was not able to do it properly because I had to shower and was told by the Mohs doctor not to get the wounds wet.

I'M ALIVE HURRAY

My life is easier because the nurse comes every morning. Its pretty funny how I think my life is easier with all of this going on. That is pretty funny!

And I am so excited because my internist wrote a letter to get a service dog for me. He thought it was necessary. I'm lonely and depressed, and an adorable dog companion filled with unconditional love would make me happy.

I have to send my thanks to, Myra Crane, who I love so much. She has been one of my closest friends. We met years ago and spent much time doing doggy playdates with her dog and mine. She will help me when and if I do get a dog. .

I'M ALIVE HURRAY

Count Your Blessings

Count your blessings instead of your crosses;
Count your gains instead of your losses.

Count your joys instead of your woes;
Count your friends instead of your foes.

Count your smiles instead of your tears;
Count your courage instead of your fears.

Count your full years instead of your lean;
Count your kind deeds instead of your mean.

Count your health instead of your wealth;
Love your neighbor as much as yourself.

Author Unknown

I'M ALIVE HURRAY

I'm Alive Hurray!

I Love That Line

I was very sick for about a year and the first time I took the Long Island Railroad to Penn Station my beautiful daughter Donna drove me to the station with my walker.

"How are you going down the steps with the walker?" She said.

"Don't worry I said," and asked a young man to carry my walker down.

I didn't have time to get a ticket so I was going to pay the conductor and ask for change of a $20 bill. He did not have change, but said he would be back. He looked at me and asked if I knew how old he was.

I said, "No."

He said, "I'm 50 years old."

I said, "You look very nice."

"I have a son."

I said, "You look so young."

I'M ALIVE HURRAY

He kept looking, and I knew he was waiting for me to tell him how old I was.

So I said, "I really can't tell you how old I am because I have lied so much, I really don't know."

He said, "I love that line. I'll be back with change," and he left.

He came back in a while and immediately said again, "I love that line."

I said, "I have another line for you."

"When I go to a doctor and he asks how tall are you? I always say, "I used to be 6 feet tall!"

He said, I love that line too! You are not going to pay for the ticket."

I said, "Thanks," and the train stopped.

Donna said, " That had never before happened on the Long Island Railroad."

I'M ALIVE HURRAY

Old age is no place for sissies.

Bette Davis

Epilogue

Thanking G-D and Leon for Help

I wasn't going to talk about the diabetes 2 that I have been living with for about 25 years. All five of my siblings died from some way that the diabetes affected them.

Teddy died when he was not yet fifty years old. We had a major problem when he was put on life support. And we were told that he was brain dead. We had to speak to Rabbis and learn if we could take him off life support.

The Jewish law does not allow that. Shloima my older brother insisted that his Rabbi said that we could not do it. I was waiting to hear what our Rabbi would say, but before we could make a decision Teddy died. So I sat Shiva for the third time, for my mother, my father and Teddy.

I'M ALIVE HURRAY

I have had ups and downs with diabetes for all those years. I was very careful with my diet because I was able to control my sugar intake with little help for a few years. At first, I was careful and scared that I had diabetes. For the first few years, I would handle it. Then I was put on Metformin pills for the diabetes.

Donna married Leon and he became my internist. He was proud of me for quite a while, but then I got a little careless with the way I cheated and ate some foods that diabetics, should not eat. Leon monitored my diabetes which was a serious problem, during my surgeries and Lymphoma Cancer. I have to thank G-d and Leon who kept me alive. It was a very difficult time. But again, I was able to cope and to say, "I'm Alive, Hurray!"

Today I am talking, walking, exercising, driving, and writing. I was not able to drive for over a year. I discovered a new passion as a short-story writer. I have also learned how to use an Apple Computer, and how to back-up using TIme Machine and USB pen drives. I am becoming computer literate, click by click.

Thank you all who did so much to help me with what help I needed. With love, visits, good wishes, gifts and flowers. I needed what you all did, and thank each one of you and will always feel something very special for every one of you. What a blessing that my beloved daughter Donna calls me every day. My hero, Dr. Leon Schwechter and G-d were by my side in every medical crisis.

This book's message is to say to everyone that the best way to overcome life's obstacles is with laughter and love. And thanks to my wonderful publisher, Sharon Esther Lampert, who encouraged me and helped me through the writing, editing, and publishing process. I am going to include her as my adopted grandchild, because I really do love her!

I thank G-D and pray for my family, children, grandchildren, and great grandchildren, extended family and many friends. I would never skip my praying and thanking G-D for his help. I know that I get strength from my prayers.

With Laughter and Love,
Esther Tulkoff

I'M ALIVE HURRAY

ALL YOU GET FOR NEGATIVITY IS
NOTHING

Sharon Esther Lampert
Poet, Philosopher, Peacemaker, Prophet, Prodigy

I'M ALIVE HURRAY

Appendix

Appendix

- Bubbe Esther's Daily Action Plan
- Bubbe Esther's Self Help
- Bubbe Esther Is Driving Again
- Bubbe Esther's Gluten Free Shabbat Cholent
- Join Our Club and Share Your Story

I'M ALIVE HURRAY

Bubbe Esther's Daily Action Plan

Bubbe Esther's Daily Action Plan
Today's Date: _____

LUVU
Sharon Esther

75-85
24/7 Doctors,
Disease, and
Dying

85-90
New Life
Chapter
Short Story
Writer

95-100
Famous
Writer

100-120
Break a
World Record
& Immortality

- ❏ 1. Listen to APPLE ITUNES Opera
- ❏ 2. Take Supplements
- ❏ 3. Check SUGAR
- ❏ 4. VITAMIX Green Drink
- ❏   Celery, Spinach, Kale, Cucumber
- ❏ 5. Check POOP? (Drink Water)
- ❏ 6. Eat PROTEIN:
      Eggs ❏ Peanut Butter ❏
      Sardines ❏ Protein Power ❏
- ❏ 7. Snacks:
      Apples ❏ Olives ❏
      Celery ❏ Red Peppers ❏
- ❏ 8. Practice Piano for FINGERS
- ❏ 9. Write Short Story & Back-Up
- ❏ 10. GYM (wear HURRAY t-shirt)
- ❏ 11. Socialize
- ❏ 12. TED.com (learn something new)

I'M ALIVE HURRAY

Bubbe Esther's Self Help

Bubbe Esther's Self Help

1. Eat as many green vegetables as possible.

2. Buy a blender. I use Vitamix.

3. Be happy. Make jokes.

4. Go to YouTube to find funny stuff, like Myer's 80th birthday (hilarious). The video is also on my website.

5. Appreciate what you have.

6. Take your physical therapy sessions seriously.

7. Problems you can't fix — just do the best you can!

8. Try to do something you like.

9. Love your family.

10. Everyday is a gift. Enjoy it.

I'M ALIVE HURRAY

Bubbe Esther Is Driving Again

Thank You Toyota Norman Frantz

I have been an Al Hendrickson Toyota customer for many years, and have always appreciated Norman Frantz, the service advisor. He is very nice and helpful. He has been especially nice during my long illnesses. He has always been thoughtful and caring.

I told him I might thank him if I could. He is a special employee of Toyota of Coconut Creek, Florida.

Thank you Norman Frantz for helping me be happy that I purchased the Prius from Toyota. Best wishes to you and Toyota.

I'M ALIVE HURRAY

Bubbe Esther's

Gluten Free Shabbat Cholent

Bubbe Esther's Gluten-Free Shabbat Cholent

Etymology: cholent (or sholen) from the Hebrew she'lan, which means, "that rested [overnight]."

Cholent is a traditional Jewish stew. It is simmered overnight for 12 hours and eaten for lunch on Shabbat. The pot is brought to a boil on Friday before the Sabbath begins, and kept on a blech or hotplate.

Main ingredients: meat, potatoes, beans, and barley

Gluten Free: Substitute buckwheat for barley

Step 1.
In slow cooker, add potatoes, onion and meat.
Spinkle with pepper.

Step 1. Ingredients
2 potatoes
1 onion
½ to 1 pound beef
Sprinkle pepper

Step 2.
Add buckwheat and beans on top.
Add seasonings.
Sprinkle paprika and salt.

Step 2. Ingredients
Beans:
¾ cup buckwheat
⅓ cup kidney beans
⅓ cup navy bean
Any bean you like

Step 3.
Add water to cover ingredients.
Cook on low for 12 to 15 hours
Stir occasionally.
Add more water if necessary.

Seasoning:
3 cups chicken broth
2 tablespoons honey
2 tablespoons paprika
Sprinkle salt

I'M ALIVE HURRAY

Bubbe Esther's

Join Our Short Story Club

and Share Your Story

Join Our Short Story Club
Share Your Story

I'M ALIVE HURRAY

The cathartic experience of writing is a deeply emotional process that allowed me to process the pain, heal my broken heart, and move forward and toward a fresh start and begin a new life chapter.
FEEL TO HEAL!
Laughter and Love,
Esther Tulkoff

E-mail story to: esther@esthertulkoff.com

One Mitzvah Can Change The World Two Will Make You Tired

Mitzvah: Hebrew for Good Deeds

© 2018. All Rights Reserved. Esther Tulkoff, I'M ALIVE HURRAY

Share your story...

_____

_____

_____

_____

_____

_____

_____

_____

_____

_____

_____

_____

_____

_____

E-mail to: esther@esthertulkoff.com

© 2018. All Rights Reserved. Esther Tulkoff, I'M ALIVE HURRAY

Notes

Rave Reviews

"Your book kept me laughing
from cover to cover,
though I did shed tears."
Florence Spiro

"Once I picked up the book,
I could not put it down!"
Judy Leitman

"I read the book in one sitting.
One page I was teary.
Another page I cried."
Leah Grossman

I'M ALIVE HURRAY

I'm always so happy when the children come to visit that I put $5 into the TZEDAKAH* box. And when they leave, I put in $10.

Laughter & Love
Esther Tulkoff

TZEDAKAH* Yiddish for charity

Esther Tulkoff
Last Will and Testament Digital Assets Addundum
August 1, 2018

1. (Bubbe) Esther Tulkoff, of Deerfield Beach, Florida being of sound and disposing mind, do hereby make, publish and declare this addendum to bequeath my digital assets be attached to be my Last Will and Testatment.

2. Posthumously, I want the copyright of my book entitled, " I'M ALIVE, HURRAY" to be bequeathed to my publisher, Sharon Lampert; and the revenue from the book and contractual agreement to be divided equally and distributed to my two great grandchildren who were born at the same time that my book was published, July-August 2018. Namely, my great grandaughter Meira Malka Schwechter and great grandson David Myer Schwechter. Every year, my digital-assets addendum will be revised to include newborn great grandchildren:
- 2019: Great-granddaughter Navah Rachel Kalish

3. Posthumously, I want my digital assets of my book, website, social media accounts, and YouTube videos related to my book entitled, "I'M ALIVE HURRAY" to be bequeathed to my publisher and digital-assets executor Sharon Lampert.

4. Posthumously, I want all of my literary publications, first and second draft edited copies, and handwritten manuscripts to be donated to a literary library or museum achive for safekeeping for eternity. I give permission for a non-profit foundation to be set up to advance the literary arts of short story literature.

5. Posthumously, if there are any photos that I have neglected to include in my digital book, I give permission to revise my book to include missing beloved family photographs.

6. Posthumously, if there are any letters that I have neglected to include in my digital book, I give permission to revise my book to include missing beloved family letters.

7. Posthumously, on my birthday and yarzeit, I am requesting that my family come together for readings of my short stories; and listen to recitations of my online YouTube videos. You have my permission to add family photographs from these annual literary gatherings to my book.

8. Posthumously, I ask each and every generation to include my digital-assets addendum in their Last Will & Testament for eternity.

I Love Each of You Best!
Laughter and Love,

Gam zeh l'tovah

This is also for the good. (Talmud, Taanit 21a)

Nachum, a great sage who was Rabbi Akiva's teacher was nicknamed Ish Gamzu, the Gamzu man, because no matter what happened, he would say about it, **"This is also for the good."** He experienced a lot of what looked to other as very bad things- illness, misfortune, suffering.